S~~t~~ ~~College~~
Secondary Education
Columbia, Missouri 65201

Relevance and the Social Studies: A Conceptual Analysis

Curriculum Resource Center
Dept. of Education
Columbia College
Columbia, Missouri

WITHDRAWN

Relevance and
the Social Studies:
A Conceptual Analysis

Robert F. Madgic, Ph.D.

Curriculum Resource Center
Dept. of Education
Columbia College
Columbia, Missouri

LEAR SIEGLER, INC./FEARON PUBLISHERS
Belmont, California

v 300.7
M 264r

Copyright, © 1973, by Lear Siegler, Inc./Fearon Publishers, 6 Davis Drive, Belmont, California 94002. All rights reserved. No part of this book may be reproduced by any means, nor transmitted, nor translated into a machine language without written permission from Fearon Publishers.

ISBN-0-8224-5840-3.

Library of Congress Catalog Card Number: 73-77590.

Printed in the United States of America.

For

Diane, Jennifer, Kirk, and Douglas

CONTENTS

PREFACE

As I was preparing some material for a workshop on individualized education, the principal came to me with a special request: "Please don't use the word *relevance*. The teachers have heard that word too often. We want to find out what to do!"

The problem posed here is not the plea for greater relevance that teachers have heard incessantly in recent years. We have here the case, so typical in education, of a concept too vague to guide action.

This book contributes to the resolution of the problem in two ways. First, it instructs the reader in methods of conceptual analysis by having him follow one conceptual study, step by step. One purpose of this book, then, is to teach the educator a methodological approach to problem solving. In this case the problem is a conceptual one, and the method is conceptual analysis.

The second purpose of the book is to present the results of conceptualizing kinds of relevance in social studies, and show the reader how these results can guide action. The concepts of a profession are its instruments. The more sophisticated these concepts are in their development, the more effective should be their operations.

Robert F. Madgic
Los Altos Hills, California

ACKNOWLEDGMENTS

There were several persons who contributed greatly to this book, although all of its deficiencies are of my own making. I am indebted to the following scholars for their support of this project: Jan L. Tucker, D. Bob Gowin, Lawrence G. Thomas, Richard E. Gross, Leonard Wax, and Mary Willis.

Chapter 1

The Problem with Relevance

"Can a man such as George Washington really be relevant to the 'Now' generation?"[1]

Innumerable questions such as this one have recently been raised—and left unanswered—in the context of the social studies. The problem is *relevance*.

Presumably, relevance connotes some readily identifiable objective that should be considered by curriculum planners, classroom instructors, textbook authors, or whoever may be trying to revitalize the curriculum. Educators, however, have proved themselves adept at ascribing multiple meanings to the term. In the following pages, we will try to sort out these meanings and pin them down.

The following examples illustrate the problem that relevance presents as an educational concept.

Example 1

Take Carole Batten, a 23-year-old brunette I met recently. "It's too bad second-graders can't protest," she says. My kids protest already, I argued, but she had something else in mind—the terrible frustration children experience today of having to conform to education that is often irrelevant. Not only does this frustrate seven- and eight-year-olds, but it is a large part of what is firing other students to protest throughout the world.

Carole hopes that some of the rigidity of the classroom will be broken up by the coming of teaching machines and advances in audio-visual education, for example, video tapes. But more encompassing is her hope that education for all students—second graders, undergraduates, graduates—can move more effectively toward relevancy. "It's time children started having science experiments in the streets."[2]

1

Discussion. Regardless of whether one agrees or disagrees with this explanation of the origin of student protests, what does this statement contribute to an understanding of educational relevance? How can an educational planner "move more effectively toward relevancy?" By holding science experiments in the streets? It is hard to believe that the problem of relevance could be solved so simply. If we abandon the classroom, does the curriculum suddenly take on relevance?

Example 1 illustrates how a term can be given the main responsibility for defining a problem (irrelevance), and its solution (relevance), although its specific implications remain obscure. Without clarification, this passage communicates little.

Example 2

A supervisor goes to observe an American history class. The teacher devotes the entire period to a discussion on the war in Viet Nam. The supervisor has observed this teacher five times, and each time the class session has been devoted to a current events topic. In response to the supervisor's query on why some of the historical questions are being neglected, the teacher replies, "Those questions aren't relevant to these kids. I try to focus on subjects that are relevant."

Discussion. Equally disconcerting as the first example are the uses of relevance illustrated here. Relevance is now being equated with currency. As a result, current events have become the sole focus for social studies instruction in this class. Should every curriculum planner delete all historical topics from course outlines as the teacher did in Example 2? If so, there will soon be many historians out of work. Surely, currency and relevancy are not synonymous.

A second disturbing aspect of the teacher's reply is his use of relevance alone as the basis for curricular decisions. Does relevance *per se* possess the conceptual clarity and strength to justify choosing one strategy over another? At best, this history teacher's claim of relevance provides a point of departure for launching a thorough examination of instructional objectives—objectives that are not supplied by the mere claim of relevance.

Example 3

An article in *Social Education* entitled "Chicago's Center for Inner City Studies: An Experiment in Relevance"[3] contains five references to the term *relevance:*

A. Amidst the controversy over community control, student rebellion, tenant strikes, welfare rights, gang warfare, black power, urban renewal, and relevant scholarship is Chicago Center for Inner City Studies, a branch of Northeastern Illinois State College.

B. What emerges from classroom and faculty seminars is the notion that a relevant curriculum is not only timely but timeless: that its timelessness lies greatly in its spirit of creativity, resourcefulness and idealism, for concepts may be learned and quickly outdated but learning to conceptualize is a facility which defies both the cultural and the generational gap.

C. The special relevancy of dance to the black community underscores the advantages of beginning the education process where the community is, and thereby facilitating the deepening and broadening of the knowledge base.

D. Perhaps the most relevant aspect of the Center for Inner City Studies is its direct involvement with one of the most burning issues of our times: the polarization of the races.

E. The result is a daring and unprecedented experiment in relevancy.

Discussion. Example 3 illustrates still more disparate uses of relevance. The article presents several uses of the concept and implies all of them simultaneously. No explanation is given for these different implications.

The title itself—"An Experiment in Relevance"—implies that the term *relevance* communicates specific meaning by itself. But an analysis of the uses in the article implies otherwise.

Paragraph (A) does not communicate any particular instructional strategy or specific meaning. But (B) suggests that "a relevant curriculum" is "learning to conceptualize," and it places no restrictions whatsoever on the content or context selected.

From (C), we can infer that a relevant education is one that begins "where the community is." It suggests that the curriculum planner should choose instructional strategies related to community activities, such as dances performed in the black community.

In (D), the curriculum planner is encouraged to look to current issues ("the polarization of the races," for example) for the source of relevant curriculum content. And (E) resembles both (A) and the title usage, implying that the term can be used independently of other references.

The uses of *relevance* in this example indicate that the term cannot be associated with only one instructional strategy. Three different strategies are suggested here, all supposedly involving relevance. Multiple implications arising from uses of a term are not inherently misleading, but confusion arises when the multiple implications are not intended or acknowledged.

Example 4

A. Any specialized knowledge is more meaningful, more relevant, if presented in its historical context.[4]

B. Somewhat existentialist is today's child. He is interested in the here and now; to him the present is far more relevant than the past or the future.[5]

Discussion. The conceptual confusion about relevance is underlined in these two uses that focus on the place of history in the social studies curriculum. Here the concept of relevance is invoked both in support of and opposition to the study of history. In neither case is it clear what the writer means by *relevance*.

Example 5

A. What seemed relevant then to the people being studied may have as much relevance for the future as what seems relevant to us now.[6]

B. Unfortunately, we often resolve this problem by teaching most thoroughly those periods of history which are most remote from our students, and of least relevance to the situations which they will face as adult citizens.[7]

C. Obviously, a great amount of the history of the human race does not bear on possible present-tense generalizations (that is, present outlooks), including those which serve the natural interest of students. It is only necessary that the generalizations be shown. . . . Probably certain events of the fourth century B.C. are more relevant to several large issues today than most of the "news" reported in current-events classes.[8]

Discussion. The uses cited here focus more on the question: *How can history be made relevant?* than on the question: *Is history relevant?*

In (A), the author identifies the interests of people from a past era as a source of data relevant to the future of the student. But his meaning of relevance cannot be distinguished from that of the author in (B). These two examples further illustrate how relevance is used without explanation to justify particular social studies curricula.

Paragraph (C) states a specific relationship between historical data and present-tense generalizations. Although one possible relationship within a study of history is broadly identified, the precise elements of that relationship are not provided. The key for determining what makes one historical study *relevant* and another one *irrelevant* is still missing.

Reviews similar to this one on history could be made for other issues in the social studies (the relevance of the social sciences, for example) to further illustrate the problem of conceptual confusion about relevance. But here it is sufficient to make the point that the term *relevance* does not clarify either issues or professional communication.

Because claims and justifications based on relevance are capable of affecting outcomes (the choice of curriculum), as in the case of the history teacher who chose to focus almost exclusively on current events, the concept is worthy of rigorous analysis. As the basis for our inquiry, we can pose the following questions: *Does the concept* relevance *hold multiple meanings and implications for theory and practice in social studies education? If so, what happens to social studies curriculum and instruction if one kind of relevance for social studies is accepted rather than another?*

One place to begin searching for answers to these questions is in the attempts others have made to clarify the implications of educational relevance.

Notes

1. Susan Ludel, "Portrait of an Old Revolutionary," *TV Guide,* 19 April 1969, p. 12.
2. John J. Veronis, "The Beautiful Ones," *Careers Today,* 1968, p. 2.
3. Sonja H. Stone, "Chicago's Center for Inner City Studies: An Experiment in Relevance," *Social Education,* May 1969, pp. 528–532.
4. Walter Rundell, Jr., "History Teaching: A Legitimate Concern," *Social Education,* December 1965, p. 522.
5. Glenys Unruh, "Urban Relevance and the Social Studies Curriculum," *Social Education,* October 1969, p. 708.
6. William Cartwright, "Selection, Organization, Presentation, and Placement of Subject Matter in American History," *Social Education,* November 1965, p. 538.
7. James M. Wallace, "Making History Relevant," *Social Education,* January 1962, p. 17.
8. Maurice P. Hunt and Lawrence E. Metcalf, *Teaching High School Social Studies* (New York: Harper & Row, 1968), pp. 149–150.

What's Been Done about the Problem

The problem of educational relevance has two dimensions. On the one hand, many educational programs are plainly missing the mark. Recognizing this, critics have filled numerous books with insights on what is wrong with our schools. At the local level, students have expressed their demands for greater relevance through varied forms of protests. *Irrelevance* has become synonymous with all that is wrong with the schools, and *relevance* has become the desired solution.

But before we can initiate vital educational reforms, we must answer the following questions: What is the proper mark? What are the desirable focuses for school programs? The clarification of educational relevance must precede constructive change. It is this aspect of the problem that will be of concern to us here.

The search for an acceptable definition of educational relevance has been widely pursued. Innumerable commentators and scholars have attempted to pin it down. Fred W. Friendly, Professor of Broadcast Journalism at Columbia University, offered the following definition of relevance in an address to the National Council of Teachers of English in 1968:

> Relevance is simply the interconnection between history and/or literature and what one scholar calls the "significant pursuit of the confirmation of today's reality."[1]

One difficulty with this statement is that it focuses only on history and/or literature. Why can't chemistry have relevance? The precise aspects of the elements to be connected by relevance, moreover, are left unspecified. It is clear that this definition is both too restrictive and too general to be of much help.

6

Historian Henry Steele Commager has this to say about relevance:

A relevant experience is overwhelmingly subjective. It happens to each individual as new worlds open up—falling in love, having a child, hearing the beauty of a Mozart sonata. The university creates an environment where the whole of the present, past and future can be relevant. It finds a place for Inca ruins, for music, for the great problems of science. It creates an atmosphere where the students can decide what is relevant to them.[2]

In contrast to Friendly's statement, Commager is saying that everything and anything can be relevant to any given person. If this analysis were satisfactory, then nothing further would need to be clarified. Each person would be allowed to discover relevance on his own. There may be considerable merit in Commager's explanation, but it does not clarify the multiple uses of relevance we found in Chapter 1.

In his book *Schools Without Failure,* psychiatrist William Glasser devotes one chapter to educational relevance. In summary, he writes:

Thus we have both parts of relevance:

1. Too much taught in schools is not relevant to the world of the children. When it is relevant, the relevance is too often not taught, thus its value is missed when it does exist.
2. The children do not consider that what they learn in their world is relevant to the school.

Relevance, the blending of one's own world with the new world of school probably is poorly established for most students.[3]

Glasser thus views relevance as the blending of two worlds—the world of the students and the world of the school. According to this formula, the ultimate relevance would be a total merging of school and community. One might ask, why even have schools? Do not the purposes of schools involve more than the child's immediate experiences? Although Glasser may have identified a worthwhile instructional strategy, it can be viewed as only one of many possibilities.

Social Studies Educators and Relevance

Social studies educators have been quite attentive to the prevailing confusion regarding claims of relevance or irrelevance. However, many attempts to clarify the implications of relevance have been undertaken within the narrow conceptual framework of the common dictionary meaning of relevance—"relation to the matter at hand."*

---

*For instance, see Massialas's and Cox's treatment of "the criterion of relevance" in their discussion of the reflective classroom in *Inquiry in Social Studies.* Also, see Oliver and Shaver's discussion of the factors of relevance in *Teaching Public Issues in the High School.*

In some cases, though, the analysis of relevance has gone beyond the dictionary definition and has begun to reveal far richer implications for education. One treatment which imparts substantive significance to the analysis of relevance is found in a journal article by social studies educators Metcalf and Hunt entitled "Relevance and the Curriculum." In a section on the concept of a relevant curriculum, they write:

> What can education do these days that would be relevant? We suggest that the schools incorporate in their curriculum a study of an important social movement, rejection by youth, and that this study emphasize examining, testing, and appraising the major beliefs caught up in this movement. . . . We need the kind of educational relevance that would help and require young people to examine their most basic assumptions about the kind of world that exists, and how they propose to change the world from what it is into something preferable.[4]

Here Metcalf and Hunt have identified two dimensions to "educational relevance"—a content dimension ("an important social movement, rejection by youth"), and a process dimension ("emphasizing examining, testing, and appraising the major beliefs"). But the precise components of curriculum relevance are not the important consideration at this point. Rather, we are investigating the idea that *relevant curriculum* is a concept that possesses substantive and clear educational meaning. As we learned in Chapter 1, this idea has not yet been clarified.

Another attempt to explain the implications of relevance for social studies can be seen in the following analysis by Cuban:

> As I use it, relevance refers to tapping students' experiences through examples taken from popular TV programs, current music, dance steps, language, and public issues—kids do discuss intensely, and earnestly, crime, the draft, Vietnam and riots. Relevance also refers to learning style, that is, using techniques that play to the strengths of youngsters as role playing, manipulating of materials, moving from the specific to the general. Relevance refers to children's feelings—knowing that hate, anger, love, fear, self-esteem, power are universal emotions and concerns and offer excellent opportunities to examine peoples and times far removed from the street corner.[5]

Here Cuban has identified three dimensions of relevance—students' experiences, learning style, and children's feelings. The first is similar to, but broader than, Metcalf's and Hunt's reference to an important social movement. The second is similar to their cognitive dimension, but the third represents a new dimension—children's feelings.

These two examples suggest that some social studies educators believe that there is more to educational relevance than its dictionary usage. But thus far, only vague suggestions have been offered.

Extended Treatments of the Problem

A few of the more extensive and perceptive analyses of educational relevance also pertain to our problem.

In the preface to *Education for Relevance: The Schools and Social Change,* the authors state:

> The thesis of this book is clearly that education, to be anything important, must touch the lives of men; hence the title, *Education for Relevance.* . . . Meaningful education must make contact with cultural values, social functions, and individual lives.[6]

Later in the book, they explain educational relevance in these terms:

> The relevance of education is its capacity to help students learn how to influence their own future instead of resigning themselves to supposed inevitabilities. To meet this test of relevance, the schools must teach the methods to appraise intelligently the claims of those who shout "Impossible, it cannot be done!"[7]

In these brief references, several focuses for relevance are suggested. From the title, for instance, we can infer that "social change" is the critical variable. However, the authors go on to introduce "cultural values, social functions and individual lives," and in the second excerpt, "influence" over the future and "methods" of appraisal. Clearly, the authors recognize the possibility of multiple focuses for educational relevance. They even identify specific variables. However, the fact that each of these variables requires separate consideration is not mentioned. Rather than pose this as the important problem and proceed to analyze the alternative implications, the authors accept the presumed integrity of educational relevance. It is up to the reader to infer the alternatives.

Green's Classification Schema. In a paper on the problem of relevance in the university,[8] Green presented a classification schema on "useful distinctions" concerning relevance in education. His classifications are based on five claims that he said, "might be made when it is declared that education is irrelevant or that it should be relevant." His categories and their definitions are as follows:

Personal relevance: Claims made in the first person about the relevance of education to the speaker.

Programmatic relevance: Claims concerning the relevance of educational content to specific vocational goals or to an understanding of important social problems.

Institutional relevance: Claims about the relevance of institutions or organizations to their goals.

Relevance of the educated man: Claims that education is irrelevant to the "real world."

Moral relevance: Claims that education is irrelevant to the worth of a man.

In order to derive these categories, Green most likely considered the claims of relevance that he had heard, and reduced them to his five summary kinds. Making the claims explicit in the form of questions would lead to the following:

1. How relevant is education to me? (*personal relevance*)
2. How relevant is the educational program to: (a) vocational goals? (b) important social problems? (*programmatic relevance*)
3. How relevant is the institution to its goals? (*institutional relevance*)
4. How relevant is education to the "real world?" (*relevance of the educated man*)
5. How relevant is education to the worth of a man? (*moral relevance*)

A close inspection of these claims reveals the differing bases upon which they are made. In (1), Green is interested in who is making the claim. In (2) and (3), he is interested in an analytic relationship between variables. In (4) and (5), he is interested in the validity of these claims. Although Green does not explicitly treat the differences among these starting points, it is important that we note them. Not only do they support the hypothesis that there are multiple kinds of relevance in education, but they also suggest the kinds of questions that might be raised in analyzing claims of relevance in social studies.

Fantini and Weinstein's Levels of Relevance. A different approach to the clarification of relevance in education has been presented by Fantini and Weinstein.[9] In response to the question, *What is relevant?* they write that "there seem to be at least four causes of irrelevance in education, and consequently, four levels on which relevance may be achieved." Their four levels are:

1. Teaching procedures may be irrelevant to learning styles.
2. Subject matter may be irrelevant to the learner's knowledge of his physical realm of experience.
3. What is taught and how it is taught may be irrelevant to the learner's feelings.
4. What is taught and how it is taught may be irrelevant to the learner's concerns.

This classification schema identifies variables within education that can be related by the concept of relevance. On one side of the possible relationships, we have teaching procedures and material or content. On the other side, we have learning styles, learner's knowledge, learner's feelings, and learner's concerns. This analysis of relevance is limited, however, by the authors' own bias, seen in their prescription that education ought to move "from an emphasis solely on cognitive, extrinsic content to an equal emphasis on affective, inner content."[10]

Further, their sole focus for relevance is the learner. They do not allow for the possibility of focuses such as social issues—a focus chosen by Metcalf and Hunt, and by Cuban. In fact, Fantini and Weinstein conclude their analysis of relevance by offering the following definition:

> It is our general hypothesis that relevance is that which connects the affective, or feeling, aspects and the cognitive, or conceptualizing, aspects of learning.[11]

By limiting their focus and presenting a narrow definition of relevance, Fantini and Weinstein have restricted the potential richness of their conceptualization. However, their work is valuable as a further example of how the fields of education can be mapped out *vis a vis* the problem of relevance.

Henze's Kinds of Relevance. A penetrating analysis of relevance unrelated to any particular context is provided by Henze.[12] His stated objective is to examine how relevance functions in the first step of every sort of informal argument in "deciding which facts are relevant to the issue at hand." Henze thus restricts his analysis right at the outset to a particular function of relevance, namely, establishing the relationship of facts to an issue.

This function resembles the dictionary use of relevance. Henze describes his task as that of determining the kinds of relationships that exist between facts and issue, and how they are established. He identifies five kinds of relationships:

1. *Relevance:* an analytic relation between a statement of the issue and statements of alleged facts, for example, whatever "statements of fact" can be deduced from a statement (or statements) of the issue or which follow necessarily from the definitions of any terms used in stating the issue.
2. *Relevance:* a causal relation between properties or circumstances.
3a. *Relevant:* whatever (belief) affects the attitudes of a person; whatever (reason) makes a difference to a man's judgment.
3b. *Relevance, psychological:* a linguistic interpretation.
4. *Relevant:* whatever ought to make a difference to the attitudes of a person.
5. *Relevance:* a verbal performance.

Henze terms these five kinds of relationships analytic, causal, psychological, normative, and performative, respectively.

In a discussion of how relevance is determined in the contexts of law, art, and morals, Henze concludes that practicality prevails, even in legal cases. He decides that the concept of relevance "can, perhaps, be analyzed best as a practical not a theoretical concept; i.e. by noting how it operates in arguments, not by using it to understand how arguments operate." According to him, facts are open rather than finite; relevance makes issues as well as relates facts to an issue; and expressions of relevance will depart from its dictionary usage.

Henze's conclusions are more useful to us than his list of specific kinds of relevance. His conclusions that relevance makes issues as well as relates facts to an issue suggest that relevance can serve additional functions, yet the reader doesn't really know what these functions are until he examines the term to see how it is used.

Henze's analysis suggests that an appropriate method of analyzing the concept of relevance in social studies is to examine how the term actually functions in the context of social studies education. This is the method we will investigate in Chapter 3.

Notes

1. Fred W. Friendly, *The Present-minded Professor,* A Ford Foundation Reprint (New York: Ford Foundation Office of Reports), pp. 3–4.
2. Henry Steele Commager, as quoted in *Palo Alto Times,* 23 October 1969.
3. William Glasser, *Schools Without Failure* (New York: Harper & Row, 1969), pp. 52–53.
4. Lawrence E. Metcalf and Maurice P. Hunt, "Relevance and the Curriculum," *Phi Delta Kappan,* March 1970, p. 359.
5. Larry Cuban, "Yet to be Taught: The Teacher and Student as Slow Learner," *Social Education,* February 1970, p. 149.
6. H. C. Hunt, C. G. Wrenn, V. C. Morris, S. A. Kirk, W. Van Til, and P. R. Hanna, *Education for Relevance* (New York: Houghton, Mifflin Co., 1968), p. vii.
7. *Ibid.,* p. 172.
8. Thomas F. Green, "The Concept of Relevance in Education—Some Useful Distinctions," unpublished paper, 1969. (Remarks delivered to the American Philosophical Association, New York City, 1969).
9. Mario D. Fantini and Gerald Weinstein, *Toward a Contact Curriculum* (Anti-Defamation League of B'nai B'rith), pp. 50–55.
10. *Ibid.,* p. 50.
11. *Ibid.,* p. 55.
12. Donald F. Henze, "The Concept of Relevance," *Methodos,* 13, 4950 (1961): 11–23.

Chapter 3

How Can the Educator Analyze His Concepts?

Concepts are tools essential to any professional endeavor. The clearer the implications of a concept, the more distinct should be the practices which stem from them. The professional educator can sharpen his concepts, the tools of his trade, by subjecting them to rigorous analysis. This chapter briefly outlines some methodological considerations for the benefit of the social studies educator who wishes to learn how to go about the analysis of a concept such as *relevance*.

Philosophy As Analysis

Henze's analysis can be adopted as a point for beginning our analysis of concepts. He writes that the concept of relevance "can, perhaps, be analyzed best as a practical not a theoretical concept; i.e. by noting how it operates in arguments, not by using it to understand how arguments operate."[1] This approach stems from a philosophical position referred to as ordinary language philosophy.

The procedures implied by ordinary language philosophy are known as informal analysis, as opposed to formal analysis. Formal analysis stresses the formulation of a technical or artificial language to solve philosophical problems, but the "essence of the informalist view is that natural language has the most power to remedy its own deficiencies."[2] According to this philosophical position, the way to understand and resolve problems is "to determine how our language is in fact used."[3]

Two main philosophical groups have practiced ordinary language philosophy. The first group, following the beliefs of Wittgenstein, a twentieth century philosopher, takes the position that philosophical problems should be solved through the usage of the ordinary language that causes the problems. The second group includes Ryle, Austin, P. F. Strawson, and others associated with Oxford. This group has been "more interested in the details of ordinary language and in drawing general philosophical conclusions."[4]

Ryle addressed himself to the concept of *use* as the key word in the phrase "the ordinary use of the expression." His approach emphasizes how a concept or object is used, rather than how it is defined. Ryle claims it is erroneous to study the *meaning* of an expression because that would imply that one expression is related to another by something contained in the verb *to mean.*

An emphasis on use directs attention to "the teachable procedures and techniques of handling or employing things, without suggesting unwanted correlates."[5] It also permits us to speak of mismanaging, mishandling, and misemploying concepts. We can say that a certain expression is being used in an absurd fashion, but we cannot necessarily say that the expression has an absurd meaning.

In summary, the ordinary language philosophers assert that philosophical problems arise because of the uses of ordinary language, rather than because of an inadequacy intrinsic to the language itself. The way to resolve philosophical problems, then, is to examine the problematic expression in a variety of contexts, rather than to examine the expression itself in isolation.

According to ordinary language philosophers, philosophy is not a set of doctrines but rather a process of analysis. To philosophize, therefore, is to clarify given concepts in the context of their disciplines.

Conceptual Analysis

Having accepted the view that philosophy is the process of analysis, our next task is to identify methods of conceptual analysis. What procedures and methods can we employ in analyzing concepts?

Analysis has no *a priori* form or method *per se.* The problem at hand establishes the framework for analysis, so different problems will require different analytic approaches. There are some general techniques of analysis, however, that can be described.

According to Kneller, one approach to the solution of a philosophical problem is first to note the words and expressions that are involved in the problem.[6] The analyst then examines various uses of each word or expression in order to determine the uses that make the most sense. Finally, the analyst examines the philosophical problem before him to see how the words and expressions are being used. The analyst will attempt to show that the problem exists, not because of the inability of ordinary language to express the meaning, but because words and expressions are being used in ways which are not appropriate.

A tool of analysis basic to the procedure outlined here is the identification of paradigm cases. This is achieved by referring to the standard uses of an expression—uses that are normal and customary. Other uses of the expression can then be compared and contrasted to the paradigm to determine whether or not they are standard.

Related to the identification of paradigm cases is the technique of presenting exemplary instances of a word or expression in given contexts. In some instances, these uses can be clear cases of inappropriate or nonstandard uses, as well as appropriate ones. Exemplary cases can and should illustrate a variety of uses so the differences can be fully clarified.

It is not always possible to find exemplary cases for a given term. In this instance, the analyst might construct or invent cases in order to show how the word or expression could be used. This process, however, has to be evaluated with the objectives of the analysis in mind. If the actual uses of a term are under investigation then the invention of cases would not be appropriate.

Another analytic strategy involves asking questions that precede the central inquiry. This technique can clarify thinking that might remain clouded if the central question were dealt with directly. Soltis utilizes this strategy when he confronts the question, "What is the definition of education?"[7] Instead of trying to answer this question immediately, Soltis raises two prior questions: What is meant by a definition? How many kinds of definitions are there? This strategy may temporarily swerve the inquiry away from the central question, but it should clarify both the nature of the problem and that of the inquiry process itself.

At this point, we can raise some prior questions about conceptual analysis: How does a concept differ from a word or a term? How does one move from word definition to conceptual analysis? What is meant by conceptualization?

Kaplan focuses on the specifics of moving from terms to concepts.[8] He explains that one utterance resembles other utterances and that when grouped together, several utterances can be identified as a term. Similarly, the entire range of uses of a term may be said to constitute a usage of the term that serves as a norm. The term has meaning through its family of meanings—that is, the relatedness of each of its several uses.

A person's interpretation of the meaning of a term is a *conception*. In Kaplan's words, a set of conceptions is a *concept*. A concept is an impersonal and timeless construct. But Kaplan points out that as conceptions change, so will the concept.

Conceptualization is an organizing process that permits a particular phenomenon, such as a use of the term relevance, to be viewed as part of a larger group rather than as a unique instance. It is a process that we impose on phenomena as a means of bringing order to their occurrences.

Conceptualization and concepts, therefore, serve a normative function in that they identify how the world ought to be organized. The meaning of each concept, however, is determined by its context and by the way each user interprets it.

Where Does Meaning Reside?

The discussion of how concepts are formed, and for what purposes, gives rise to the prior questions: How does one locate the meaning of a concept? What, in fact, is meant by *meaning?* Several different approaches can lead to answers to these questions. It is important that we sort them out and adopt one that is valid for clarifying the possible meanings of relevance in education.

One approach is to assume that a term stands for something that exists apart from the term itself. According to this view, a term is used to represent some distinct quality or quantity, and the task is to locate this true meaning of the term. We can safely predict, however, that several meanings with shades of differences will be uncovered by the person who wishes to say conclusively, "This one is the true meaning." How do we choose?

Another approach to meaning is simply to define a term oneself, or go to a dictionary for its meaning. But here a prior question can be asked: What does it mean to define a term? At this point, we can turn to Scheffler, who has done some pertinent work with definitions.[9] Scheffler has identified three types of definitions—descriptive, stipulative, and programmatic.

A descriptive definition, according to Scheffler, is a literal attempt to describe the term, either its characteristics or its use. Obviously, if a term has several uses, then it also has several descriptive definitions, one for each use or set of characteristics. Because a descriptive definition attempts to portray something at the most commonly accepted level, it usually involves the least disagreement. An example of a descriptive definition of relevance is its dictionary definition: "relation to the matter at hand."[10]

A stipulative definition is one that the user either adopts or gives, saying "This is the way I will use the term." The user controls the use of the term so that no disagreements occur over its meaning. This is not to say that everyone has to agree with his definition, but at least everyone knows (or is supposed to know) how the term is being used. Many of the explanations or definitions of relevance fall into this category. For example, a superintendent of a school district defined relevance in the following terms: "Relevant education is teaching youngsters a method of inquiry, and teaching them how to inquire for facts to solve problems."[11]

Scheffler calls his third kind of definition programmatic. This form contains prescriptive elements and often communicates how something should be. Whereas a stipulative definition represents a personal or individualistic view, a programmatic definition presents a meaning that is, in the view of the user, a standard or norm: "This is the meaning that this term ought to have."

The following proposal incorporates many elements of Scheffler's programmatic type of definition:

> What can education do these days that would be relevant? We suggest that the schools incorporate in their curriculum a study of an important social movement, rejection by youth, and that this study emphasize examining, testing, and appraising the major beliefs caught up in this movement. . . .
> We need the kind of educational relevance that would help and require young people to examine their most basic assumptions about the kind of world that exists, and how they propose to change the world from what it is into something preferable.[12]

Accepting Scheffler's kinds of definitions, one might use them to account for the various uses, and hence meanings, of relevance. The location of meaning as presented in a definition is in the person who takes the responsibility and the control for defining the term. In each of Scheffler's three cases, however, meaning is static.

Another approach to the location of meaning lies not in deciding how a term is defined, but how it is used. In this case, the investigator examines the ways and contexts in which a term is used rather than looking at its stated meanings. The assumption underlying this approach is that the test of meaning is pragmatic—it lies in experience. This approach recognizes that the meaning of a term may change as it is used in new ways. Here, meaning is dynamic, not static.

Yet another test for meaning can be applied by asking: What difference does the definition of a term make? If a term is defined or used in one way rather than another, what are the consequences? We can theorize, for example, that acceptance of one meaning of relevance will lead to one outcome, and acceptance of another meaning to another outcome. In other words, if a person wanted to uncover the precise meaning of relevance in a given context, he would look at the outcome of its use. So, in answer to the question, *How does one locate the meaning of a concept?* we find we can choose among several approaches.

Implications for Social Studies

From the discussion of philosophical and conceptual approaches, we can identify several methods that are valid for the task of analyzing kinds of relevance for social studies.

The approach that views the meaning of a concept as a static truth labeled with a name has little to recommend it. For our purposes, the more promising method appears to be the one that investigates the actual uses of a concept. Philosopher P. F. Strawson has stated the rationale for this approach simply but cogently: "To observe our concepts in action is necessarily the only way of finding out what they can and cannot do."[13]

There is considerable merit in the approach that looks to outcomes as the source of meaning because actions are generally more telling than words. In social studies education, these outcomes would be the actual curricular practices resulting from choices among relevance alternatives. There is a practical limitation to this method, however, because the analysis *per se* cannot be described before the outcomes have occurred.

The analyst takes the task of language clarification and attempts to teach that term so that others will know what they can and cannot do as a result of his analysis. Concept analysis is teaching, and just as in teaching where each student is different and requires individual strategies, so, too, in concept analysis, the problem itself outlines the tasks and the methods.

Notes

1. Henze, *op. cit.,* p. 21.
2. George F. Kneller, *Logic and Language of Education* (New York: John Wiley & Sons, 1966), p. 169.
3. V. C. Chappell, ed., *Ordinary Language* (Englewood Cliffs, N.J.: Prentice-Hall, 1964), p. 2.
4. *Ibid.,* p. 3.
5. *Ibid.,* p. 29.
6. Kneller, *op. cit.,* pp. 173–174.
7. Jonas F. Soltis, *An Introduction to the Analysis of Educational Concepts* (Reading, Mass.: Addison-Wesley, 1968), pp. 2–7.
8. Abraham Kaplan, *The Conduct of Inquiry* (San Francisco: Chandler, 1964), pp. 46–52.
9. Israel Scheffler, *The Language of Education* (New York: Charles C. Thomas, 1960), Chapter I.
10. Webster's Seventh New Collegiate Dictionary (Springfield, Mass.: G. and C. Merriam Co., 1967).
11. As quoted in *Palo Alto Times,* 16 April 1969.
12. Metcalf and Hunt, *op. cit.,* p. 359.
13. P. F. Strawson, quoted in Kneller, *op. cit.,* p. 171.

Chapter 4

Analyzing Relevance and Its Uses

The dictionary use of relevance implies a relationship between two variables. Once a subject has been identified, the task is to decide if a given variable is related to it. *Relevant* is used in everyday discourse to stipulate this kind of connection between variables. Neither the kind of relationship, nor the nature of the variables is important—only the existence of a relationship matters.

The etymology of relevant, however, suggests another usage that might differ from the dictionary one in appearance, although not necessarily in intent. *Relevant* stems from the Latin *relevare,* meaning to raise up, to lift. The term relevant, therefore, can be used to elevate a given variable and to indicate that it stands out in some way. This use recognizes that the variable in question is relevant; similarly, to say that the variable is irrelevant is to say that it need not be recognized.

The use of relevance prompts the raising of prior questions: Can something be independently relevant, or must certain conditions be present first? If the latter, then what kind of conditions? In other words, does relevance have to be set within a context before its meaning is clear? A framework for answering these questions has been provided by Kaplan.

Kaplan's Openness of Meaning

The essential characteristic of relevance can be related to what Kaplan refers to as "openness of meaning,"[1] an expression "for any respect in which the specification of meaning of a term leaves its usage uncertain."[2]

Kaplan finds four kinds of openness of meaning: systemic openness, vagueness, internal vagueness, and dynamic openness. On systemic openness he writes: "There are many terms whose meaning can be specified only as they are used together with other terms, or in full sentences."[3] Their meaning depends not on one isolated example, but on the "context of the whole set of sentences in which they appear," because only as we encounter the term in more and more contexts of varying sorts do we come to understand it more fully."[4] Such a term may legitimately possess diverse meanings.

On the characteristic of vagueness, Kaplan writes that "all terms are to some degree vague, that they *must* be vague, is apparent just from the way in which we learn to use language."[5] He considers vagueness to be a necessary condition of terms.

Concerning internal vagueness, Kaplan points out that it is difficult to identify the ideal case which a given term represents. The very task assumes that there is a spectrum of cases from marginal to standard or ideal. This characteristic can be contrasted with external vagueness that involves deciding whether or not something belongs to a particular class. With internal vagueness, the task is to decide where a particular case stands with regard to the ideal.

The fourth category is dynamic openness. Kaplan defines this quality as "the permanent possibility of change in meaning by terms."[6] As terms are used in new contexts, their meaning is also capable of changing.

Kaplan's attention to the openness of meaning for some terms has direct application to our analysis of relevance. For example, in many cases the meaning of relevance presented in social studies contexts is vague. In addition, one use of relevance may vary so widely from another that a spectrum of meaning exists (internal vagueness), and an ideal use cannot be identified. Relevance also possesses dynamic openness because its precise meaning and implications depend upon the full context of its use.

In summary, however, we find that Kaplan's systemic openness is the one most applicable to our analysis of relevance in the social studies. Although relevance is used with vagueness, and although its meanings (usages) vary from context to context, in the final analysis the word must be examined in connection with other terms.

Relevance as an Educational Slogan

At this point, it is helpful to consider three theoretical uses of relevance:

>   A. Relevance exists.
>   B. This is relevant.
>   C. This is relevant to that.

Only in case C is a relationship between two variables clearly demonstrated. Case A, on the other hand, conveys the least specific meaning. Simply to claim relevance is to communicate little unless one variable can be seen to possess a relationship to some other variable. Given the context, one may be able to infer the respective references and draw the relationship, but however obtained, this additional information is necessary for any meaning to be conveyed.

Case B, like case A, is incomplete. The second of the two references is missing here. This case exemplifies the etymological basis of relevant, because a given variable is being elevated to a position of prominence. But even here the identification of prominence requires a context—prominent next to what, or under what circumstances? The second variable must still be specified.

Cases A and B both fit another pattern of usage which can be described as slogans. Many statements involving uses of relevance in the context of education fall into this category.

Scheffler writes that slogans "make no claim either to facilitate discourse or to explain the meaning of terms."[7] The statements *social studies education should be made more relevant* and *these social studies materials are relevant* conform to this description. Scheffler does point, however, to the practical purport of slogans that, within particular contexts, convey practical messages in spite of their literal vagueness. This dimension is also apparent in slogan uses of relevance—there are many practices in social studies education being advanced in the name of relevance. In other words, use of a concept as a slogan is apt to produce effects, but if the meaning of the concept is not clear, then its effects on social studies instruction will not be clear, either.

Komisar and McClellan have also analyzed the characteristics and possible effects of slogans.[8] They have drawn two conclusions: (1) slogans do not imply particulars, and (2) they are systematically ambiguous. Komisar and McClellan further analyzed how slogans can take on meaning:

> But slogans need not remain in such a useless state. Slogans may come to summarize some definite set of particulars. That is, in our term, it can come to acquire in *interpretation.* . . . Much of the accepted activity of educational debate and discussion is to establish and disestablish standard interpretations of certain slogans. Educators spend a good deal of time attempting to capture slogans for one set of proposals rather than for another.[9]

Komisar and McClellan believe that slogans can come to be associated with particulars and specific proposals. But what kinds of particulars in social studies education are being communicated by the use of *relevance?* Is the term interpreted in one way only? Or does it imply a variety of proposals? If various sets of proposals are being advanced, then they should be made explicit in order to clarify professional communication and discourage slogans.

An Analysis of Social Studies Uses of Relevance

Up to this point, we have identified several characteristics of the term relevance. According to standard usage, relevance serves a connective function, either explicit or implicit, between two variables. Part of the task of understanding or clarifying a use of relevance, therefore, is to identify the variables that the term connects.

We have found that some uses of relevance conform to the description of an educational slogan. One way to determine whether relevance is being used as a slogan is to check whether variables are present, even implicitly, in the context of the use. If none can be found (Case A), or if only one is present (Case B), then it is likely to be a slogan. Whether a specific interpretation accompanies the usage can be determined only if curricular outcomes can be found.

The open-ended characteristic of a slogan allows a person to assign his own variables to the term. In this way, a variety of outcomes can result from a single use of relevance. In order to locate meaning in a slogan in the absence of specific variables, then, we must look at the practical outcomes. If the outcomes are consistently the same, then apparently the slogan has taken on a single interpretation. Practical outcomes, however, are difficult to determine. They require investigations to be conducted over time and in a number of places.

We can now describe the initial set of tasks in our analysis of relevance as a concept in social studies education. First, we must identify clear uses* of relevance in context. Next, we must identify the variables that *relevance* connects. In the following pages, we will examine forty-four uses of relevance. Each use is followed by a diagrammatic structure showing the variables immediately preceding and following the reference to relevance. If variables are missing ($-$), it means that they could not be identified and thus represent case A or B examples.

1. It is countered here that chronological history easily degenerates into a mere chronicle of names, dates, and events, many of which have no relevance to the present or the future. . . ."[10]

---

*In order to secure a comprehensive set of social studies uses of relevance, the author investigated printed sources that altogether comprise a wide-ranging documentation of social studies education. Sources on the fringe of the context of social studies were also examined in order to insure the richest possible examples of uses of relevance. A "use" was defined as a sentence containing a reference to *relevance*, or *irrelevance*, plus the immediately surrounding sentences. This permitted the references to be inferred if necessary, yet provided sufficient limits to restrict subjective interpretations.

Diagrammatic structure: chronicle of names, dates, and events/irrelevant/present, future

2. With greater concern for the future, we might begin to consider that behavioral characteristics have relevance for citizenship in the past, present, and the future. (As distinct from the *what* should be taught issue.)[11]

Diagrammatic structure: behavioral characteristics/relevant/citizenship

3. Any specialized knowledge is more meaningful, more relevant, if presented in its historical context. Few ideals, concepts, phenomena spring, like Athena, full blown from the brow of Zeus. They develop in a time sequence, which is to say historically.[12]

Diagrammatic structure: specialized knowledge/relevant/(—)

4. There were other manifestations that the course was relevant. One of the commonest signs was frequently expressed through regrets at not having more time on units of study and requests for a year-long course. Students disciplined each other—better order than usual and criticism of those who didn't read the material or participate. Pupils in one class came to audit another and students from one semester sat in on second semester classes.[13]

Diagrammatic structure: course/relevant/students

5. Recognizing that the consumers in this appropriately consumer-oriented enterprise are heterogeneous, young, and characteristically self-centered, it seems reasonable to assume that the problem of motivation will be dealt with effectively in proportion as the materials used have readily apparent relevance to their personal situations.[14]

Diagrammatic structure: materials/relevance/personal situations

6. The process which thoughtful educators follow in drawing the line between relevant and irrelevant knowledge is as follows: (1) a core of pervasive human problems is identified and, (2) a number of concepts and relationships which purport to explain and illuminate the problems are emphasized and serve as organizing principles in the selection of content.[15]

Diagrammatic structure: knowledge (concepts and relationships)/relevant/human problems

7. Some of the content we are now teaching would acquire meaning if its relevance to current problems and issues were perceived by students. Some of the content has no such relevance, and should be replaced by content that does. This principle does not mean that history has no value unless it is modern history. Some of the most rele-

vant content for understanding contemporary society is to be found in the histories of Greece and Rome. A teacher can use the content of history and social science as evidence within a reflective process that tests propositions and clarifies conflicts.[16]

Diagrammatic structure: content/relevance/current problems

8. Difficulty in handling World History. Reasons: "First, history piles up, so to speak, at a prodigious rate. New, relevant, and significant material clamor for consideration. To ignore them in history courses would be to cheat youth of a knowledge of the most exciting part of its heritage.[17]

Diagrammatic structure: material/relevant/(—)

9. Unfortunately, we often resolve this problem by teaching most thoroughly those periods of history which are most remote from our students, and of least relevance to the situations which they will face as adult citizens.[18]

Diagrammatic structure: periods of history/relevant/situations they will face as adult citizens

10. In order to make World History relevant to mid-twentieth-century American students we employ the flashback technique which directly relates the past to the present.[19]

Diagrammatic structure: world history/relevant/mid-twentieth-century American students
and
past/relevant/present

11. The pupil should be helped to think about the ideas he has picked up in his secondary environment (non-home environment). He may then be expected to emerge from the social studies classroom with tested ideas that are relevant to the nature of the social order.[20]

Diagrammatic structure: ideas/relevant/nature of social order

12. I propose that any attempt to make a study of the past relevant to the needs of the present must raise questions with which we are presently concerned. Can a teacher of history make the issues of Socrates' death or of Thoreau's refusal to pay taxes or of John Brown's trial relevant to his students (and therefore *worth* the study) without raising fundamental questions about man's responsibilities to his state and to his conscience?[21]

Diagrammatic structure: study of the past/relevant/needs of the present

13. In consequence, social studies educators are caught between uttering commitments to education for rational citizenship and perpetuating

curricula which are based on criteria that seem in large part irrelevant to this objective. . . .[22]

Diagrammatic structure: curricula/irrelevant/education for rational citizenship

14. It is not surprising that questions about the rationale for social studies instruction are rarely raised in the heat of teaching. By default, a curriculum is perpetuated that is too often seen by students as not only lacking in challenge, but as irrelevant to the realities of life.[23]

Diagrammatic structure: curriculum/irrelevant/realities of life

15. Many non-academically inclined students will continue to be frustrated by the irrelevance to their own lives and to society's prevalent issues of much of what passes for social studies instruction; and academically able students will still be left to recognize on their own the germaneness of their studies to the contributions they could, and in many instances will, make to their society.[24]

Diagrammatic structure: social studies instruction/irrelevant/their own lives
                            and
                            social studies instruction/irrelevant/society's prevalent issues

16. Is it easier or more difficult to get ahead in America today? Sociological tools of analysis, combined with illuminating examples from U.S. history, can make this analysis meaningful, both in terms of its relevance to students and their understanding of history. Much has been said, and rightly so, regarding the absence of Negro history in many textbooks.[25]

Diagrammatic structure: sociological tools of analysis/relevance/student's understanding of history

17. I should choose instead to narrow the frame of reference and focus on one problem that is relevant, a problem that poses serious dangers to our society, particularly our young people in the "under 30" group.[26]

Diagrammatic structure: problem/relevant/(—)

18. Replacing old curriculum with new curriculum does not in itself help children to think and develop concepts concerning their relationship to their environment. The content of the material taught must be relevant to life in our changing urban society.[27]

Diagrammatic structure: content/relevant/life in a changing urban society

19. The vision of the teacher as heroic figure may be relevant to genuine inquiry. For to take inquiry seriously, he and his pupils must examine ideas in the classroom, including the teacher's and those of his pupils and their parents.[28]

Diagrammatic structure: teacher as heroic figure/relevant/genuine inquiry

20. We might even start by admitting that what we mainly know about the teaching act itself is that it can be enjoyable, exciting and compelling and that discovery may be relevant to this.[29]

Diagrammatic structure: teaching act/relevant/discovery

21. Teachers using inquiry to differentiate instruction need to believe in the capacity of children to think for themselves. They must be convinced that the freedom to think and autonomy in thinking are the prerequisites to effective thinking. The classroom settings for inquiry most likely reflect this attribute when:

1. There is a focus on problems which are defined, probed, and labelled as relevant by the learners.[30]

Diagrammatic structure: problem/relevant/learner

22. To individualize, then, teachers need to consider each child's needs, capacity, personality and interests: to personalize, learning must be both relevant and enriching. It should be obvious that not all children will be interested in the same thing at the same time, and that "group" or "class" inquiry is virtually impossible by definition.[31]

Diagrammatic structure: learning/relevant/each child's needs, capacity, personality and interests

23. Structure belongs in the minds of teachers so that they can utilize those personal, individual, and very different experiences that are relevant to children to build broader meanings, to make connections, to see the significance of what exists in the everyday world. In order to do this, materials of all kinds are necessary; but they need not be tightly organized, predigested packages that lead down one-way paths to predetermined goals.[32]

Diagrammatic structure: experiences/relevant/children

24. The way in which this new generation looks at their nation and the world at large has very little to do with the ideological preoccupations of their elders, however relevant these may have been at one point of time.[33]

Diagrammatic structure: ideological preoccupations of their elders/relevant/world

25. Nearly all students, regardless of age or academic ability, when given the opportunity to learn about the successes and failures, the joys and agonies, the hopes and despair, the resignation and rebellion of

Asians, believe the classroom experience to be pertinent, meaningful, and relevant.[34]

Diagrammatic structure: the classroom experience (to learn about the successes and failures, the joys and agonies, the hopes and despair, the resignation and rebellion of Asians)/relevant/human experiences

26. More generally, a boy or girl will be able to play at those roles that he must play in earnest once he becomes an adult and enters the complex modern society of adults. In so doing, he learns both the intellectual skills relevant for those roles, and the moral traits—that is, the traits which schools presently attempt to inculcate under the general label of "citizenship education."[35]

Diagrammatic structure: intellectual skills and moral traits/relevant/adult roles

27. But Professor Handlin goes on to point out that young people readily learn things that seem relevant to them, even if such things are not formally taught. He instances "the lad who cannot remember the date of the Spanish-American War or the meaning of 'sixteen to one,' but who can name the pitchers in each game of the World Series of 1948 and can reel off batting averages by the yard."[36]

Diagrammatic structure: things that seem/relevant/young people

28. As pupils use their past experiences or present situations to identify problems or raise questions, the inquiry process becomes more relevant to them.[37]

Diagrammatic structure: inquiry process/relevant/pupils

29. Be relevant. Involve the children in constructive community activities and studies.[38]

Diagrammatic structure: teaching/relevant/constructive community activities and studies

30. Social studies teachers must promote this identity quest by encouraging black pupils to inquire into the extent to which racism has permeated our written history and our society, to become familiar with the contributions that black people have made to American life, and by developing more positive attitudes and higher expectations for black youth. Making the social studies curriculum more relevant for the black pupil is imperative if we are to help mitigate the mounting racial crisis in our cities and help the black child gain a more positive "self."[39]

Diagrammatic structure: social studies curriculum (to enquire; to become familiar; to develop more positive attitudes)/relevant/black pupil

31. In an effort to make lively and relevant the search for meaning in the social studies, it is well to keep in mind four leading principles concerning the choice and presentation of subject matter.[40]

Diagrammatic structure: search for meaning/relevant/(—)

32. Using the method of inquiry, which has been described, facts would always be taught in relationship to other meaningful facts which are relevant to the goal to be achieved. Facts would be used in establishing generalizations right now and this is the way the student would learn. They would not be stored away for use at some future date. Utility and relevance to the student would be apparent as the facts learned would hence always be accompanied by understanding and purpose.[41]

Diagrammatic structure: facts/relevant/goal to be achieved

33. Unfortunately—and what follows here is of special relevance for today's student population, searching as it must for moral and ethical guidelines which are relevant to its particular rendezvous with history—a large proportion of the traditional values and norms of behavior that directed preindustrial societies are not necessarily relevant to our own day. Evidence abounds that morals are far from absolute. To take a random example, slavery was held to be moral. . . .[42]

Diagrammatic structure: what follows/relevance/today's student population
and
moral and ethical guidelines/relevant/its particular rendezvous with history
and
traditional values and norms of behavior/irrelevant/values and norms of behavior of our own day

34. And since history is not a record of continual success, any inquiry into the causes of decay may lead properly to a re-examination of the values which motivated people in the past in order to determine whether these values have vitality and relevance when applied to the conditions of society today.[43]

Diagrammatic structure: past values/relevance/conditions of society today

35. Clearly, the making of decisions among the alternatives listed above is essentially a matter of sorting out and applying facts until a conclusion is reached which honestly and accurately summarizes all facts that are relevant to the problem.[44]

Diagrammatic structure: facts/relevant/problem

36. What emerges from classroom and faculty seminars is the notion that a relevant curriculum is not only timely but also timeless; that its timelessness lies greatly in its spirit of creativity, resourcefulness, and idealism, for concepts may be learned and quickly outdated but learning to conceptualize is a facility which defies both the cultural and the generational gap.[45]

Diagrammatic structure: curriculum/relevant/learning to conceptualize

37. All that is needed is for teachers and curriculum developers to begin to understand what the notion of a planetary society means. They will find an adequate number of opportunities to plug relevant concepts into existing courses, and students will begin to acquire some of the perspectives they will need to function as citizens of a world society.[46]

Diagrammatic structure: concepts/relevant/perspectives needed by citizens of a world society

38. The team arrived at an operational definition of a generalization: for the purposes of this series of studies a generalization is a universally applicable statement at the highest level of abstraction relevant to all time or stated times about man past and/or present, engaging in a basic human activity.[47]

Diagrammatic structure: universally accepted statement/relevant/all times; basic human activity

39. Somewhat existentialist is today's child. He is interested in the here and now; to him, the present is far more relevant than the past or the future. He can be more readily motivated when he senses a problem.[48]

Diagrammatic structure: present/relevant/today's child

40. In order to teach about the world system we must first be able to think and talk about the world as a whole; and to do this, we must have available a repertoire of relevant concepts and a vocabulary of appropriate symbols.[49]

Diagrammatic structure: concepts/relevant/world as a whole

41. Still others blame the emphasis on history for the social studies program's inability to make the study of man and society relevant to the interests of today's youth.[50]

Diagrammatic structure: study of man and society/relevant/interests of today's youth

42. A second school of thought, while sharing some of these same values, claims that the ultimate purpose of the social studies is not inquiring within social science, but informed decision making in society at large. Although they do not deny the relevance of certain inquiry skills and analytic methods of the social sciences to that end, proponents of this second school of thought marshall impressive evidence for the premise that social science understandings do not, of themselves, guarantee transfer to the decision-making requirements of the citizen.[51]

Diagrammatic structure: inquiry skills and analytic methods of the social sciences/
relevant/informed decision making

43. The scholastic method of breaking it down into feasible parts helps to clarify the problem: What other problem is it like? How is it like the present experience being analyzed? How is it different? Does any aspect of its difference require that the problem be approached in a way other than from that of the present experience? By this method, the student can see the relevance of asking the right questions. Here they apply the skills of locating and organizing information.[52]

Diagrammatic structure: asking the right question/relevant/(—)

44. If familiarity with the history of our country is needed to provide an understanding and appreciation of our indigenous institutions, if a knowledge of our history is necessary for us to understand our present and to help us shape our future, then it is imperative that the nature and relevance of economic forces and institutions, as they have evolved, be an integral part of the course in U.S. history.[53]

Diagrammatic structure: economic forces and institutions/relevant/understanding
and appreciation of our indigenous institutions

A Descriptive Framework

The preceding uses of relevance can now be collectively described by listing each of the variables related to relevance. This descriptive framework can be presented as follows:

Variables Related By Relevance

Antecedent	Subsequent
chronicle of names, dates and events	present—future
behavioral characteristics	citizenship
specialized knowledge	personal situations
course	human problems
materials	current problems
concepts and relationships	situations they will face as adult citizens

Antecedent	Subsequent
content	mid-twentieth-century American
periods of history	students
world history	nature of social order
ideas	needs of the present (questions with
study of the past	which we are presently concerned)
curricula	education for rational citizenship
curriculum	realities of life
social studies instruction	their own lives
search for meaning	student's understanding of contempo-
history	rary society
facts	student
moral and ethical guidelines	today's student population's rendezvous
past values	with history
education process	conditions of society today
universally accepted statements	problem
(generalizations)	where the community is
present	perspectives needed by citizens of a
study of man	world society
inquiry skill and analytic methods of the	all times; basic human activity
social sciences	today's child
social studies curriculum teaching	world as a whole
inquiry process	interests of today's youth
things that seem	informed decision making
intellectual skills	black pupil
learning about successes	constructive community activities and
and failures, the joys	studies
and agonies, the hopes	pupils
and despair, the	young people
resignation and	adult roles
rebellion	learning to conceptualize
ideological preoccupations of their	discovery
elders	children
teaching act	each child's needs, capacity, personality
experiences	and interests
learning	learner
problems	genuine inquiry
teacher as heroic figure	life in a changing urban society
sociological tools of analysis	student's understanding of history
asking the right questions	skills of locating and organizing in-
economic forces and institutions	formation
	understanding and appreciating our in-
	digenous institutions

Our task now is to move from this framework of specific references to
a more generalized framework.

Notes

1. Kaplan, *op. cit.,* pp. 63–70.
2. *Ibid.,* p. 63.
3. *Ibid.,* p. 63.
4. *Ibid.,* p. 64.
5. *Ibid.,* p. 64.
6. *Ibid.,* p. 66.
7. Scheffler, *op. cit.,* p. 36.
8. Paul Komisar and James E. McClellan, "The Logic of Slogans" in B. Othanel Smith and Robert H. Ennis, eds., *Language and Concepts in Education* (Chicago: Rand McNally & Co., 1961).
9. *Ibid.,* pp. 201–202.
10. William H. Cartwright, "Selection, Organization, Presentation, and Placement of Subject Matter in American History," *Social Education,* November 1965, p. 538.
11. Albert H. Yee, "Preparation for the Future," *The Social Studies,* January 1968, p. 21.
12. Walter Rundell, Jr., "History Teaching: A Legitimate Concern," *Social Education,* December 1965, p. 522.
13. Walter H. Langhorst and John L. Sullivan, " 'Hey, That's Me!' A Relevant Course," *The Clearing House,* December 1968, p. 205.
14. Thomas F. Powell, "Reason and Necessity in the Social Studies," *Social Education,* December 1963, p. 432.
15. Byron G. Massialas, "Revising the Social Studies: An Inquiry-Centered Approach," *Social Education,* April 1963, p. 185.
16. Lawrence E. Metcalf, "Some Guidelines for Changing Social Studies Education," *Social Education,* April 1963, p. 198.
17. A. Wesley Roehm, "More About Less Versus Less About More in World History," *Social Education,* April 1960, p. 163.
18. James M. Wallace, "Making History Relevant," *Social Education,* January 1962, p. 17.
19. L. S. Stavrianos, "New Viewpoints in Teaching World History," *Social Education,* March 1962, p. 131.
20. Robert E. Jewett, "The Importance of Teaching the Social Studies in an Age of Science," *The Social Studies,* October 1961, p. 166.
21. Bernard Feder, "A Study of the Past Focused on the Present," *Social Education,* October 1968, p. 531.
22. James P. Shaver, "Social Studies: The Need for Redefinition," *Social Education,* November 1967, p. 589.
23. *Ibid.,* p. 592.
24. *Ibid.,* p. 592.
25. William M. Hering, Jr., "Social Science, History, and Inductive Teaching," *Social Education,* January 1968, p. 37.
26. Lloyd Meeds, "Education: Key to the Drug Problem," *Social Education,* October 1969, p. 664.

27. Yetta M. Goodman, "Metropolitan Man and the Social Studies," *Social Education,* October 1969, p. 702.
28. Martin LaForse, "Why Inquiry Fails in the Classroom," *Social Education,* January 1970, p. 67.
29. *Ibid.,* pp. 67, 81.
30. Thomas N. Turner, "Individualization Through Inquiry," *Social Education,* January 1970, pp. 72–73.
31. Vincent R. Rogers, "A Macrocosmic Approach to Inquiry," *Social Education,* January 1970, p. 75.
32. *Ibid.,* p. 77.
33. His Excellency Soedjatmoko, "A Foreign Visitor's View of the United States; Stereotypes and Realities," *Social Education,* July 1969, p. 790.
34. Robin J. McKeown, "Developing Asian Studies Program Materials," *Social Education,* July 1969, p. 844.
35. Samuel Brodbelt, "Simulation in the Social Studies: An Overview," *Social Education,* February 1969, p. 177.
36. Charles G. Sellers, "Is History on the Way Out of the Schools and Do Historians Care?" *Social Education,* May 1969, p. 511.
37. Dorothy J. Skeel and Joseph G. Decaroli, "The Role of the Teacher in an Inquiry-Centered Classroom," *Social Education,* May 1969, p. 548.
38. Edward G. Ponder, "Some Psycho-Social Phenomena of the Disadvantaged and Social Studies Learning," *Social Education,* January 1969, p. 65.
39. James A. Banks, "Relevant Social Studies for Black Pupils," *Social Education,* January 1969, p. 69.
40. Ivor Kraft, "Social Studies: The Search for Meaning," *Social Education,* November 1967, p. 597.
41. Harris L. Dante, "The Humanities, History, and the Goals of the Social Studies," *Social Education,* May 1967, p. 403.
42. Alastair M. Taylor, "Today's Students in Tomorrow's World," *Social Education,* November 1966, pp. 507–508.
43. A. Wesley Roehm, "The Teaching of Contemporary Affairs: A Teacher's Point of View," *Social Education,* November 1966, p. 514.
44. Shirley H. Engle, "Decision Making: The Heart of Social Studies Instruction," *Social Education,* November 1960, p. 303.
45. Stone, *op. cit.,* pp. 529–530.
46. Howard Mehlinger, "Enlarging the International Component of the High School Curriculum," *Social Education,* November 1968, p. 685.
47. Paul R. Hanna and John R. Lee, "Content in the Social Studies," *Social Studies in Elementary Schools,* ed. John U. Michaelis, Thirty-Second Yearbook, National Council for the Social Studies, 1962, p. 73.
48. Unruh, *op. cit.,* p. 708.
49. Lee F. Anderson, "An Examination of the Structure and Objectives of International Education," *Social Education,* November 1968, p. 643.
50. Mindella Schultz, "The Place of History in the Social Studies Program," *Social Education,* December 1968, p. 794.
51. Charlotte Crabtree, "Supporting Reflective Thinking in the Classroom,"

Effective Thinking in the Social Studies. ed. Jean Fair and Fannie R. Shaftel, Yearbook, National Council for the Social Studies, 1967, pp. 79–80.

52. Kopple C. Friedman and William E. Muller, "The Problem-Solving Approach to Economics in the Twelfth-Grade Problems Course," *Social Education,* April 1966, p. 277.

53. Kalman Goldberg and Ronald W. Boehme, "Economic Education: A New Dimension in the U.S. History Course," *Social Education,* April 1966, p. 273.

Chapter 5

Categorizing the Multiple Sides of Relevance

The analysis of uses of relevance in social studies presented in Chapter 4 led to the listing of numerous antecedent and subsequent variables. Now we must translate this raw data into something more meaningful. Our task is essentially one of organizing the references to relevance according to broad patterns.

Grouping the references into more generalized categories could itself become a major conceptual undertaking if we were intent upon developing some new ways of describing educational phenomena. Because this is not the intention here, the categories will be grossly drawn and based largely on conventional categories.

Antecedent Variables

First, we will develop general categories for variables on the left side of the framework. We will refer to these terms as the antecedent variables.

A review of the list of antecedent variables reveals that a number of them refer to instructional material. These can be grouped under the heading *content.*

The variables include:

> chronicle of names, dates, and events
> specialized knowledge
> concepts and relationships
> periods of history
> world history
> ideals
> facts

moral and ethical guidelines
past values
generalizations
ideological preoccupation of their elders
problems

It is apparent that this content category itself encompasses several dimensions and can be narrowed even more. (For example, what *kind* of content does the social studies educator wish to emphasize?) For our purposes, however, the general category of content is satisfactory. A prescriptive use of relevance employing a content variable would state that some dimension of social studies content—be it specific factual material, values, ethics, or problems—should be related to one of the variables on the right side of the descriptive framework.

A second category can be formed to include variables that cluster around the subject of *teaching method.* Each of the following variables refers to the method of instruction:

search for meaning
education process
inquiry skills and analytic methods . . .
inquiry process
teaching act
problems
teacher as heroic figure
sociological tools of analysis

Here, a prescriptive statement would entail relating the method of teaching to some variable on the right side of the descriptive framework.

A third category includes all variables that refer to the *learning method.* The creation of this category assumes that teaching and learning processes are not identical or even similar experiences. As Smith points out,

That learning does not necessarily issue from teaching, that teaching is one thing and learning is quite another, is significant for pedagogical research. It enables us to analyze the concept of teaching without becoming entangled in the web of arguments about the processes and conditions of learning; in short, to carry on investigation of teaching in its own right. Teaching, like learning, has its own forms, its own constituent elements, its own regularities.[1]

Assuming that teaching and learning methods do differ, this distinction is not clear in our list of antecedent variables. These concepts need to be clarified for the betterment of professional communication and decision making in the social studies. Some of the variables, such as "search for meaning" or "education process," might refer to either teaching or learning methods, or both. The vagueness of several of the antecedent variables requires, therefore, that there be some duplication among categories. This result does not refute or even weaken our premise that the concepts of teaching and learning are distinct. As with the content category, it merely highlights the vague quality of much of the writing on education.

These references encompass learning methods:

> search for meaning
> educational process
> study of man
> inquiry of skills and analytic methods . . .
> inquiry process
> intellectual skills
> learning about . . .
> experiences
> problems
> sociological tools of analysis

A few items on the list of antecedent variables have not yet been placed in one of the three categories—content, teaching method, or learning method. These include:

> study of the past
> curriculum
> social studies instruction
> social studies curriculum

These phrases are so vague as to be of little use in communicating what should be made relevant. Either content, teaching method, or learning method might be intended by each of these phrases. If this is the case, then the three categories already formed are sufficient and inclusive. We can now represent the left side of the descriptive framework as:

> Content
> Teaching Method
> Learning Method

Subsequent Variables

Grouping the variables on the right side of the descriptive framework involves more complex judgments than grouping those on the left because of the greater variety of references. The subsequent variables answer the question, relevant to *what?* A use of relevance with both an antecedent and a subsequent reference stipulates that one of the three variables—content, teaching method, or learning method—is or should be directly related to the subsequent variable. Our next task, then, is to formulate categories that encompass the subsequent variables.

Examination of the subsequent variables suggests grouping them initially into two broad categories. Many of the variables focus directly upon *the learner*—his interests, his future, his thinking processes. The remaining variables refer generally to *conditions in the world*.

The Learner

citizenship
personal situations
situations they will face as adult
   citizens
mid-twentieth-century American
   students
rational citizenship
their own lives
student's understanding of
   contemporary society
student
today's student population's
   rendezvous with history
perspectives needed by citizens
   of a world society
today's child

interest of today's youth
informed decision making
black pupil
involvement in constructive community activities and studies
pupils
young people
adult roles
discovery
children
each child's needs, capacity,
   personality, and interests
learner
genuine inquiry
student's understanding of history

Conditions in the World

human problems
current problems
nature of social order
realities of life
conditions of society today
problem

where the community is
all times basic human activity
world as a whole
life in a changing urban society
values and norms of behavior of
   our own day

There is some room for misplacement or double usage of a few of the variables. For instance, *problem* fits in both categories. The references to the *present* or *future* could refer to either the learner's future or to future conditions in the world. The placement of a variable in either one of these groups is not the important issue. All we need to do here is identify and accept the two broad categories. Because all the variables are accounted for by the two groups, we can conclude that these categories are all-inclusive.

This division of variables is supported by Jerome Bruner, who writes in an article entitled, "The Skill of Relevance or the Relevance of Skills:"

The word relevance has two senses. The first is that what is taught should have some bearing on the grievous problems facing the world, the solution of which may affect our survival as a species. This is social relevance. Then there is personal relevance: What is taught should be self-rewarding, or "real," or "exciting," or "meaningful." The two kinds of relevance are not necessarily the same, alas.[2]

Bruner's two senses of relevance—social relevance and personal relevance—resemble our two groups, The Learner and Conditions in the World. In other words, Bruner's distinctions appear to hold up under empirical investigation, however rudimentary. But, once we accept these two broad categories, it becomes apparent that we have only scratched the surface of relevance.

The Learner. Once the two categories have been established, we can ask: What aspects of the learner should be the focus for the antecedent variables? The question leads to an inquiry into the concept of *learner* and its specific dimensions. A rigorous analysis of this concept is beyond the scope of this work, but we can go back to the references and look for specific focuses. W' can also refer to the conceptual accomplishments of others.

A number of references focus on the learner's intellectual growth, or his cognitive domain. These references include:

> student's understanding of contemporary society
> informal decision making
> discovery
> genuine inquiry
> student's understanding of history

This subcategory can be classified Learner-Cognitive, indicating that it focuses on the thinking or cognitive domain of the learner.

A second subcategory can be derived from the focuses on the non-cognitive dimensions of the learner conveyed by the terms *interest, needs,* and *personality* of the learner. Once again it can be stated that each of these concepts can itself be analyzed and conceptualized. However, it is sufficient for our purposes to identify them as belonging to the affective domain as delineated by Krathwohl et. al.[3] This second subcategory can be called Learner-Affective.

A third subcategory can be drawn from the references:

> personal situations
> their own lives
> involvement in constructive community activities and studies
> interests of today's youth

At first inspection, these variables do not appear to represent a specific dimension of the learner and may even be covered by the congitive or affective categories. Nevertheless, they represent another dimension of the learner. Cuban, in a brief analysis of relevance, suggests a possible approach to the establishment of this subcategory:

> As I use it, relevance refers to tapping students' experiences through examples taken from popular T.V. programs, current music, dance steps, language, and public issues—kids do discuss intensely, and earnestly, crime, the draft, Vietnam and riots. Relevance also refers to learning style, that is, using techniques that play to the strengths of youngsters as role playing, manipulating of materials, moving from the specific to the general. Relevance refers to children's feeling—knowing that hate, anger, love, fear, self-esteem, power are universal emotions and concerns and offer excellent opportunities to examine peoples and times far removed from the street corner.[4]

Cuban identifies three dimensions of relevance—students' experiences, learning style, and children's feelings. The latter two dimensions are related to the cognitive and affective domains repectively. The first dimension is similar to the variables we are considering for a third subcategory. These dimensions focus upon things the learner is familiar with, most generally by physical proximity. The terms *community* or his *own life* belong in this group. We will call this subcategory Learner-Contiguous Environment because the focus is on the learner's physical surroundings or what he experiences in his immediate environment.

A fourth group of variables centers on the learner's future. This focus is conveyed by the references:

> citizenship
> situations they will face as adult citizens
> rational citizenship
> today's student population's rendezvous with history
> perspectives needed by citizens of a world society
> adult roles

Most, if not all of the dimensions for the learner's future are encompassed by the expression *adult roles*. It encompasses the specific references to the learner's future responsibilities of citizenship, and his future economic (occupational) requirements. But the learner also looks forward to the assumption of many roles—marital, parental, religious, recreational. This subcategory should be sufficiently broad to include all these possibilities. We will call it Learner—Future Adult Roles.

The variables in the general category of the Learner have now been divided into four subcategories. These groups are established more for descriptive than conceptual purposes, because our intent here is to describe more clearly the field of inquiry. The outcomes of this process are the following groupings:

> Learning—Cognitive
> Learner—Affective
> Learner—Contiguous Environment
> Learner—Future Adult Roles

Conditions in the World. The second major category, Conditions in the World, can be similarly broken down into subcategories. An initial inspection of these references indicates we can make a time-oriented distinction. Several variables focus on the present or current events. Others focus on universal or timeless phenomena. One dimension of the former can be represented by the subcategory Current Social Problems and Issues, and the other can be called Universal Human Concerns. Although these subcategories are not explicit, they clearly establish the time dimension, and that is adequate for our descriptive purposes.

The time distinction between a problem of current significance (such as Viet Nam) and one of universal import (such as the rights of the individual) does not represent all of the subsequent variables under the general category Conditions in the World. The remaining variables, however, present a problem at first glance because of their pervasive vagueness (*realities of life, needs of the present, nature of the social order, life in a changing urban society*). What we need are precise expressions that represent more accurately the implications of these variables.

One concept that integrates several of the expressions is *values*. Defined simply, values are a culture's "ideals of what is worth striving for."[5] They include the ideas, norms, behaviors, and practices of a culture. Values are "the nature of the social order," if we can ascribe meaning to such a vague phrase. The subcategory Cultural Values, can thus represent a set of subsequent references with a general orientation to society.

What do we do with the references to *needs,* or *realities of life?* These transcend the categories developed thus far; they present an instrumental dimension. Their prescription is to make the antecedent variables relevant to certain requirements (needs) of the society.

An appropriate question here is: What are the requirements of society? In answer, we can cite two dimensions of society—people and institutions. Concerning the first dimension, we could say that serving the needs of the individual is the same as serving the needs of society, because society consists of individuals. If this were all that was necessary to account for the requirements of society, then the category would be covered by the focus on The Learner. But society also consists of institutions—schools, churches, businesses—that have requirements beyond those of the individual. These requirements can be called *maintenance;* that is, one dimension of the needs of society is the need to maintain institutions. This dimension becomes another subcategory, Maintenance of Social Institutions.

Summary of Grouping Procedures. The procedures we have described here involved the identification and listing of antecedent and subsequent variables related through the concept of relevance. Our purpose was to record the variables contained in actual uses of relevance.

The next procedure consisted of grouping the variables in order to achieve systematic simplicity or compactness. We made choices on the formation and labeling of the groups in an attempt to describe, not create, categories.

Using these data, we can now draw the following descriptive framework:

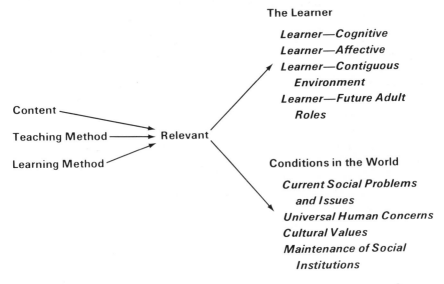

The Learner

Learner—Cognitive
Learner—Affective
Learner—Contiguous
Environment
Learner—Future Adult
Roles

Content

Teaching Method ——→ Relevant

Learning Method

Conditions in the World

Current Social Problems
and Issues
Universal Human Concerns
Cultural Values
Maintenance of Social
Institutions

Next, we will move from this descriptive framework to a conceptualization of the kinds of relationships relevance can make between the categories. Because the variables have been identified from uses of relevance in the context of social studies education, the outcome can be referred to as a conceptualization of kinds of relevance for social studies.

Notes

1. B. Othanel Smith, "A Concept of Teaching," in *Language and Concepts in Education,* ed. B. Othanel Smith and Robert H. Ennis (Chicago: Rand McNally & Co., 1961), p. 90.

2. Jerome Bruner, "The Skill of Relevance or the Relevance of Skills," *Saturday Review,* 18 April 1970, p. 68.

3. David R. Krathwohl, Benjamin S. Bloom, and Bertram B. Masia, *Taxonomy of Educational Objectives, The Classification of Educational Goals. Handbook II: Affective Domain* (New York: David McKay Co., 1964).

4. Cuban, *op. cit.,* p. 149.

5. George F. Kneller, *Educational Anthropology* (New York: John Wiley & Sons, 1965), p. 115.

Chapter 6

Kinds of Relevance for Social Studies

The procedures described in Chapter 5 led to a description of our field of inquiry—uses of relevance within the context of social studies education. The summary of uses that we made by grouping the specific references about relevance constitutes a set of phenomena that can now be analyzed and conceptualized into categories for kinds of relevance for social studies.

The results of this conceptual analysis are presented in outline form so the reader can see the schema and follow the decisions that led to its construction.

Kinds of Relevance for Social Studies

Slogan Relevance
Standard Relevance

Dictionary Relevance

Learner-controlled Relevance

Learner-centered

Psychological Cognitive Relevance
Psychological Affective Relevance
Contiguous Environmental Relevance
Future Adult Roles Relevance

Society-oriented

Public Issues Relevance
Universal Human Experience Relevance
Cultural Values Relevance
Institutional Maintenance Relevance

Non-learner–controlled Relevance

Learner-centered

Psychological Cognitive Relevance
Psychological Affective Relevance
Contiguous Environmental Relevance
Future Adult Roles Relevance

Society-oriented

Public issues Relevance
Universal Human Experience Relevance
Cultural Values Relevance
Institutional Maintenance Relevance

Self-generative Indeterminate Relevance

Slogan Relevance

Slogan uses need to be recognized as a major kind of relevance as seen in uses of the term by social studies educators. Slogan relevance is characterized by vagueness of meaning, primarily because of the lack of one or both references. The following example is one such case:

Difficulty in handling World History. Reasons: "First, history piles up, so to speak, at a prodigious rate. New, relevant, and significant material clamor for consideration. To ignore them in history courses would be to cheat youth of a knowledge of the most exciting part of its heritage."[1]

Sets of particulars or single interpretations can become associated with slogans, so their potential influence should not be discounted. For example, students may unite behind the slogan "greater relevance in education," and may achieve more control over their own educational programs as one outcome. Attachment to a vague slogan may thus lead to a state in which the particulars can then be determined.

How does one distinguish between an empty slogan and a meaningful slogan? Here the test would be in the outcomes. One would have to examine what effects, if any, a slogan has had. If it has definite outcomes—whether in the motivation of some action or in the determination of precise goals— that can be traced to a slogan, then its meaningfulness needs to be recognized. If no effects can be ascertained, then the slogan's meaning remains obscure.

When relevance is used without specifying at least one variable, then such a use can properly be labeled a slogan. However, if the term is used to communicate specific educational meaning, then it approaches the status of a concept. The conceptual schema presents evidence that uses of relevance are capable of organizing a field of data.

Standard Relevance

The second major kind of relevance in our schema is Standard Relevance. This category is based strictly on the requirement that relevance be used to draw a relationship between two or more variables in accord with its correct grammatical usage. In terms of identifying more precise categories for kinds of relevance, however, the nature of the variables is the critical area of investigation that leads to the organization of the subcategories. But first let's look at a case in which the precise nature of the variables is not the criterion.

Dictionary Relevance. Earlier, we identified one use of relevance in social studies as a dictionary use. This use is now classified as a subcategory of Standard Relevance in order to account for those uses of relevance in which the nature of the references is arbitrary rather than conforming to predetermined categories. The following use exemplifies this dictionary kind of relevance within the professional context of social studies:

> Clearly, the making of decisions among the alternatives listed above is essentially a matter of sorting out and applying facts until a conclusion is reached which summarizes all facts that are relevant to the problem.[2]

This kind of relevance, although identified here as the dictionary kind, is not as simple or straightforward as the label suggests. Henze analyzed the kinds of relationships involved in claiming that some facts are relevant or irrelevant to a problem, and how such claims are confirmed or denied.

For the purposes of our schema, Dictionary Relevance is the claimed existence of a relationship between two references, though the references themselves do not meet any particular specifications. As the descriptive framework showed, however, relevance has been used by social studies educators largely with the particular references as the essential part of the message.

Who Specifies the References for Relevance?

In examining the descriptive schema showing the variables in uses of relevance by social studies educators, a prior question can be asked: Who specifies what is relevant or irrelevant to what? Two broad categories of answers are possible—the social studies learner (the student), or a non-learner, a person who can be identified in most cases as a social studies educator.

In prescribing that an antecedent variable be made relevant to a subsequent variable, it is significant to consider who it is that will make the particular decisions. If it is a non-learner, then the assumption is that this non-learner can choose the variables that are related through relevance. We will call this broad kind of social studies relevance Non-learner–controlled Relevance.

As with Dictionary Relevance, the references for this kind of relevance do not have to conform to any prior specifications. Only the source responsible for their specification is critical here. This kind of relevance is suggested in the following use:

> Can a teacher of history make the issues of Socrates' death or of Thoreau's refusal to pay taxes or of John Brown's trial relevant to his students (and therefore *worth* the study) without raising fundamental questions about man's responsibilities to his state and to his conscience?[3]

Here, the teacher has the responsibility for deciding what social studies content is to be made relevant to the student. It is he who chooses what questions to raise and what it is about the student that will be the focus. Non-learner–controlled Relevance thus expresses the location of decision-making authority, rather than the nature of the decisions themselves.

Placing responsibility on the learner himself for the specification of relevance leads to the category Learner-controlled Relevance. In this case, the learner decides what the specifications of relevance should be. Relevance thus resides in the freedom of the learner to choose, rather than in the variables themselves. This kind of relevance is suggested by the following statement:

> Teachers using inquiry to differentiate instruction need to believe in the capacity of children to think for themselves. They must be convinced that the freedom to think and autonomy in thinking are the prerequisites to effective thinking. The classroom settings for inquiry most likely reflect this attribute when:
>
> 1. There is a focus on problems which are defined, probed, and labelled as relevant by the learners.[4]

Student demands for decision-making power within a university might be viewed as demands for this kind of *relevant* education.

Learner-centered Relevance. In reviewing the descriptive framework on generalized uses of relevance, the category of The Learner was established to encompass several of the specific references. Any one of the antecedent references—content, teaching method, or learning method—can be related to the learner. The resulting kind of relevance is Learner-centered Relevance. It differs from Learner-controlled Relevance in that the latter depends on who is at the locus of control whereas the former depends upon the focus of the subsequent references, regardless of who specifies them.

Under Learner-centered Relevance, four subcategories can be conceptualized from the possible relationships presented by the specific variables.

Learner-centered Psychological Cognitive Relevance. This use of relevance focuses on the cognitive development of the learner as the major factor in making the antecedent variables relevant. Relevant to what? Relevant to the learner's multiple thinking abilities, from simple recall to evaluation. The following use presents this kind of relevance:

> What emerges from classroom and faculty seminars is the notion that a relevant curriculum is not only timely but also timeless; that its timelessness lies greatly in its spirit of creativity, resourcefulness, and idealism, for concepts may be learned and quickly outdated but learning to conceptualize is a facility which defies both the cultural and the generational gap.[5]

The prescription implicit in this use is to make the curriculum relevant to having the learner learn how to conceptualize. The focus is on the learner, and it is specifically directed to his cognitive development.

Learner-centered Psychological Affective Relevance. This kind of relevance also centers on the psychological dimension of the learner, but here the focus shifts to his affective domain—beliefs, attitudes, values, and personality characteristics.

The following use suggests this kind of relevance:

> There were other manifestations that the course was relevant. One of the commonest signs was frequently expressed through regrets at not having more time on units of study and requests for a year-long course. Students disciplined each other—better order than usual and criticism of those who didn't read the material or participate. Pupils in one class came to audit another and students from one semester sat in on second semester classes.[6]

This use of relevance focuses on the attitude of the learner as manifested in his behavior, and leads to the designation affective, rather than cognitive.

Learner-centered Contiguous Environment Relevance. When social studies education focuses on experiences close to the learner or involving him, then another dimension is introduced. The phrase *contiguous environment* is used to express this dimension. It might encompass a variety of categories. One may focus, for instance, on a specific aspect of the learner's environment, such as his neighborhood or his family. The following use exemplifies this approach:

> The special relevancy of dance to the black community underscores the advantages of beginning the education process where the community is, and thereby facilitating the deepening and broadening of the knowledge base.[7]

This kind of relevance might also refer to more generalized aspects of the learner, as in the following:

How can the understanding of social science concepts help the slow learners to make history relevant to their lives?[8]

The reference here to "their lives" could reflect either on the learner's immediate environmental experiences or on certain of his cognitive or affective dimensions. The vagueness of the expression "their lives" makes definite identification of a kind of relevance particularly difficult here. In this case, about all one can say is that the designation Learner-centered Contiguous Environment Relevance might express the intentions of the user.

Learner-centered Future Adult Roles Relevance. This use of relevance prescribes that the antecedent variables be directed toward the future roles and responsibilities of the learner. The subsequent reference may be as vague as "situations that they will face as adult citizens." Or it may refer to specific roles, such as political or economic, in the learner's future, as exemplified by the following two uses:

With greater concern for the future, we might begin to consider what behavioral characteristics have relevance for citizenship in the past, present and the future.[9]

Recognizing that the consumers in this appropriately consumer-oriented enterprise are heterogeneous, young, and characteristically self-centered, it seems reasonable to assume that the problem of motivation will be dealt with effectively in proportion as the materials used have readily apparent *relevance* to their personal situations.[10]

The author of the second selection goes on to define "personal situations" as the roles that the learner will play as worker, consumer, taxpayer, and citizen. One could, of course, expand this list to include family, religious, and recreational roles as well. This category does not specify the adult roles to which the antecedent variables should be made relevant; it only claims that these variables can be or should be related to one or more adult roles.

A significant characteristic of Learner-centered Future Adult Roles Relevance is its clearly instrumental dimension. That is, the prescription behind this use is that one or all of the antecedent variables prepare the learner for the assumption of future roles.

Society-oriented Relevance. With Learner-centered Relevance the focus of the antecedent variables is the student—*his* psychological dimension, *his* experiences in *his* environment, and *his* future roles. As the descriptive framework shows, however, social studies uses of relevance have other focuses that can be grouped under the heading Conditions in the World. A phrase that uses this non-learner focus to describe a second broad category of relevance is Society-oriented Relevance. This kind, too, can be divided into four subcategories.

Society-oriented Public Issues Relevance. The subsequent references encompassed by this use of relevance are the issues currently before the public or the legislature. These are issues that concern all members of the society, not just one learner. In some cases, this kind of relevance is seen in reference to a specific current issue, as in the following example:

> Perhaps the most relevant aspect of the Center for Inner City Studies is its direct involvement with one of the most burning issues of our times: the polarization of the races.[11]

In other cases, the reference is to a broader range of public issues:

> Some of the content we are now teaching would acquire meaning if its relevance to current problems and issues were perceived by students.[12]

Society-oriented Universal Human Experience Relevance. Another kind of relevance can be drawn from those uses which relate the antecedent variables to universal human concerns—concerns not restricted to any one time or context. This focus is formally contained in the Stanford University studies on generalizations in the social sciences written by Paul R. Hanna and Richard E. Gross. The following statement, itself a use of relevance, presents the focus for this kind of relevance:

> The team arrived at an operational definition of a generalization: for the purpose of this series of studies a generalization is a universally applicable statement at the highest level of abstraction relevant to all time or stated times about man past and/or present, engaging in a basic human activity.[13]

This kind of relevance can also be seen in the following use:

> Nearly all students, regardless of age or academic ability, when given the opportunity to learn about the successes and failures, the joys and the agonies, the hopes and despair, the resignation and rebellion of asians, believe the classroom experience to be pertinent, meaningful, and relevant.[14]

Let's consider this latter use at greater length. The subsequent reference is not clearly specified, and the use could be identified as an educational slogan. However, the conceptual schema on kinds of relevance for social studies suggests that the writer is invoking the category of *Society-oriented Universal Human Experience Relevance* because he refers clearly to timeless aspects of the human experience. The diagrammatic structure would be: classroom experience/relevant/universal human experiences.

Society-oriented Cultural Values Relevance. This subcategory prescribes a relationship between the antecedent variables and the values of a culture or society. Although values are the determining characteristics of a culture, they are often difficult to identify because: (1) they are in a state of flux, and (2) individuals within a culture hold differing values. Consider the following use of relevance:

> A method for judgment-making should be a method of open inquiry into the relevance of values and should lead to the reconstruction of values to meet the demands of a rapidly changing world.[15]

In this use the statement "values to meet the demands of a rapidly changing world," conveys little specific meaning, although the value-centered nature of relevance is clearly being invoked.

As with the other variables that have formed the subcategories for Society-oriented Relevance, *values* can be either antecedent or subsequent references. Consider the following:

> Unfortunately—and what follows here is of special relevance for today's student population, searching as it must for moral and ethical guidelines which are relevant to its particular rendezvous with history—a large proportion of the traditional values and norms of behavior that directed preindustrial societies are not necessarily relevant to our own day.[16]

When the inquiry asks whether one variable (traditional values, for example) is relevant to a second variable (values of our own day, for example), the problem is similar to that of determining the relevance of facts to an issue in Dictionary Relevance. But the focus on cultural values has particular significance in social studies, and this is expressed by the category, Society-oriented Cultural Values Relevance.

Society-oriented Institutional Maintenance Relevance. A fourth kind of relevance for social studies within the broad category of Society-oriented Relevance can be drawn from the focus on societal needs. We have already considered the needs of the individual member of a society through the development of relevance categories under the general heading of The Learner. To serve the needs of the individual is to serve one element of the needs of society.

The second element of a society resides in its institutions. It has long been held that schools have as their primary function the transmission of culture and maintenance of societal institutions. This function, combined with the references to *needs of society,* gives rise to the category, Society-oriented Institutional Maintenance Relevance. The prescription here would be to make the antecedent variables relevant to subsequent variables designed to preserve the institutions of the society. The following use of relevance illustrates this kind of relevance:

> If familiarity with the history of our country is needed to provide an understanding and appreciation of our indigenous institutions, if a knowledge of our history is necessary for us to understand our present and to help us shape our future, then it is imperative that the nature and relevance of eco-

nomic forces and institutions, as they have evolved, be an integral part of the course in U.S. History.[17]

Self-generative Indeterminate Relevance. Thus far, kinds of relevance for social studies have been conceptualized on the basis of: (1) the locus of control, and (2) the antecedent and subsequent variables. The next kind of relevance depends on neither of these. The specific dimensions of Self-generative Indeterminate Relevance emerge from the instructional experience itself and stipulate no prior outcomes. Each participant may be affected differently.

The experience may prove to be relevant to any of several variables. For example, one learner may find one of the antecedent variables so stimulating that it becomes relevant to his affective domain, or Learner-centered Psychological Affective Relevance. Another learner may not be affected at all. A learner who decides on a particular career as a result of his study experiences Self-generative Indeterminate Relevance. In this case, a study of ancient history could be relevant to the learner's future adult roles if he chooses to become an ancient history scholar. Yet another example might be the discovery of a corrupt political practice through a study of local politics, and the resultant emergence of a public issue.

Self-generative Indeterminate Relevance can be inferred from the following statement:

> A relevant experience is overwhelmingly subjective . . . It happens to each individual as new worlds open up—falling in love, having a child, hearing the beauty of a Mozart Sonata.[18]

The relationship between two social studies variables may be consummated either at the time of the experience, or after the experience itself. The specific subsequent variable, therefore, becomes apparent sometime during or after the experience. It is important that the person intending this kind of relevance both understand its qualities and communicate his intended meaning, so that the openness is not a shield for vagueness.

The category of Self-generative Indeterminate Relevance completes our conceptual schema of kinds of relevance for social studies.

Notes

1. A. Wesley Roehm, "More About Less Versus Less About More in World History," *Social Education,* April 1960, p. 163.
2. Engle, *op. cit.,* p. 303.
3. Bernard Feder, "A Study of the Past Focused on the Present," *Social Education,* October 1968, p. 531.
4. Thomas N. Turner, "Individualization through Inquiry," *Social Education,* January 1970, pp. 72–73.

5. Stone, *op. cit.* pp. 529–530.

6. Walter H. Langhorst and John L. Sullivan, " 'Hey, that's me!' A Relevant Course," *The Clearing House,* December 1968, p. 205.

7. Stone, *op. cit.,* p. 531.

8. Allen Fredrichs, "Teacher, History and Slow Learning Adolescents," *The Social Studies,* April 1967, p. 169.

9. Albert H. Yee, "Preparation for the Future," *The Social Studies,* January 1968, p. 21.

10. Thomas F. Powell, "Reason and Necessity in the Social Studies," *Social Education,* December 1963, p. 432.

11. Stone, *op. cit.,* p. 532.

12. Metcalf and Hunt, *op. cit.,* p. 198.

13. Paul R. Hanna and John R. Lee, "Content in the Social Sciences," in *Social Studies in Elementary Schools,* ed. John U. Michaelis, Thirty-Second Yearbook, National Council for the Social Studies, 1962, p. 73.

14. Robin J. McKeown, "Developing Asian Studies Program Materials," *Social Education,* July 1969, p. 844.

15. Bernice Goldmark, "Another Look at Inquiry," *Social Education,* October 1965, p. 350.

16. Alastair M. Taylor, "Today's Students in Tomorrow's World," *Social Education,* November 1966, p. 150.

17. Kalman Goldberg and Ronald W. Boehme, "Economic Education: A New Dimension in the U.S. History Course," *Social Education,* April 1966, p. 273.

18. Commager, *op. cit.*

Chapter 7

Using Relevance to Guide the Social Studies Curriculum

This book began with the question, *Can George Washington really be relevant to the "now" generation?* Rather than attempt to answer this question immediately, we launched an analysis of the term relevance. By adopting the approach of ordinary language philosophers, and by applying methods of conceptual analysis, we developed a conceptual schema of kinds of relevance for social studies. Now we can confront the initial question armed with some analytical tools.

A first answer might be, "it all depends." The skeptic might reply, "but I could have given that answer back on page 1!"

The skeptic is, of course, correct. But now we know precisely what an answer depends on. It depends, for instance, on whether the subject of George Washington is going to be used to exemplify human ideals, or as a comparison to the national leadership of today, or to engender support for our nation's values and/or institutions. It depends on whether the experiences of George Washington can excite the imaginations and critical inspection of some youth, and on who is responsible for making those kinds of judgments. In the final analysis, it depends on whether George Washington is an appropriate subject to use in order to achieve a particular kind of relevance.

When the multiple dimensions of relevance have been clearly identified, the social studies educator has a framework he can use to analyze issues, identify priorities, and reach decisions on alternative curricular strategies. But the identification of distinct kinds of relevance does not mean that they are mutually exclusive. For example, Future Adult Roles Relevance and Institutional Maintenance Relevance may coincide if the learner is preparing for the assumption of roles vital to the maintenance of societal institutions. Public Issues Relevance may be pursued in such a way as to emphasize Psychological Cognitive Relevance. The point of the conceptual schema is not to reduce the range of choices regarding relevance, but to help facilitate decision making based on consideration of all the possibilities.

Thinking and Communication

The first area in which the social studies educator can be assisted by the relevance framework is in the clarification of his own thinking. Once this is achieved, communication will be improved. When conceptual alternatives are clearly perceived, the decision maker can weigh the various possibilities and present reasoned justifications for the stands he takes. An analysis of an example presented in Chapter 1 will illustrate this point.

In the article, "Chicago's Center for Inner City Studies: An Experiment in Relevance,"[1] the term relevance is used five times apart from the title. These uses are:

1. Amidst the controversy over community control, student rebellion, tenant strikes, welfare rights, gang warfare, black power, urban renewal, and relevant scholarship is Chicago's Center for Inner City Studies, a branch of Northeastern Illinois State College.
2. What emerges from classroom and faculty seminars is the notion that a relevant curriculum is not only timely but also timeless; that its timelessness lies greatly in its spirit of creativity, resourcefulness, and idealism, for concepts may be learned and quickly outdated, but learning to conceptualize is a facility which defies both the cultural and the generational gap.
3. The special relevancy of dance to the black community underscores the advantages of beginning the education process where the community is, and thereby facilitating the deepening and broadening of the knowledge base.
4. Perhaps the most relevant aspect of the Center for Inner City Studies is its direct involvement with one of the most burning issues of our times: the polarization of the races.
5. The result is a daring and unprecedented experiment in relevancy.

Utilizing the conceptual schema, uses 1 and 5 can be identified either as Slogan Relevance or as unidentifiable, use 2 as Learner-centered Psychological Cognitive Relevance, use 3 as Learner-centered Contiguous Environmental Relevance, and use 4 as Society-oriented Public Issues Relevance.

How should instruction be designed in order to achieve relevance? Are three different approaches intended? Should the social studies educator attempt to implement all three? Or does he consider one more effective than the others?

The idea of experimenting with different approaches to relevance is not being questioned here. But a problem arises when the experimenter does not acknowledge the different approaches he has chosen, and recognize their professional implications.

Sharpened communication is vitally important in all levels of education. For example, team teaching programs have often suffered from personality clashes or differing approaches to the subject. Perhaps what is needed are more tools for clarifying the differences among team members, and according them legitimacy. If a commitment in behalf of one kind of relevance is being questioned, then far better that the issues arise from alternative professional implications, than from questions of personality. The relevance framework helps to encourage this sort of professional dialogue.

Locus of Control

When students have voiced demands for "more relevance" in their education, often what they were challenging was not the substance of the curriculum but the decision-making processes that led to that curriculum. Students have indicated that they want more say in what and how they are called upon to learn. Thus, relevance has been equated with the locus of control for decisions.

The category of Learner-centered Relevance focuses directly on the dimensions of the individual student. Who is in the best position to identify the personal experiences, future roles, and psychological needs of that student? Should the learner be omitted from the decision-making processes that concern his own individual growth?

Typically, the locus of control over curricular decisions is in the hands of the teacher and the other adults responsible for school curricula. But certainly every person—even the youngest of children—is capable of expressing certain personal needs and interests. A child's interests, for example, would be apparent in the decisions that he makes when given a wide array of options and the freedom to choose among them. The same would hold true for the more mature student.

When student interests are ignored, a curriculum is more liable to remain static or grow stale under the weight of tradition, college entrance requirements, state codes, and adult memories than if these interests are consulted. Permitting the curriculum to be continuously tested and influenced by the persons it affects gives it a dynamic, contemporary character.

Our relevance schema draws attention to the importance of input from both students and staff by grouping the kinds of relevance under the two main headings, Learner-controlled Relevance and Non-learner–controlled Relevance. This separation should not be construed, however, as meaning that the two are mutually exclusive. An enlightened decision-making process is one that permits each of the groups to express its interests, and have them reflected in the program design. Let's take a look at some possible expressions of this commitment to learner responsibility.

In most programs, the learner is generally expected to accomplish objectives chosen by the curricular designer. Few programs consistently allow students to define their own learning objectives. To make this dimension a vital part of an educational program requires time and resources for the learner to pursue his own inquiries, and decide what interests him—what is *relevant* to him—at any given time. Here, emphasis is placed on the processes of discovery and decision making, rather than solely on a predetermined product.

Many of the organizational patterns that include non-structured dimensions in student programs (such as the informal classroom and open plan concepts at the elementary level, and variable scheduling programs at the secondary), are committed to this kind of educational relevance.

Another practical manifestation of this strategy is to present a student or a class of students with a variety of learning units or modules from which to choose. The units can be designed around relevance categories—future adult roles, public issues, or cultural values, for example. If a student's interests are not accommodated by the given units, he might be allowed to design his own unit with the guidance of the instructor. Giving each learner more responsibility for his education is an effective strategy for achieving Psychological Cognitive Relevance and Psychological Affective Relevance. Because certain kinds of relevance demand that the learner be involved and committed, any program that does not aggressively and creatively strive to achieve these goals is seriously, perhaps fatally, handicapped.

Time Considerations

In planning for relevance, the educator might well ask: When is the state of relevance to be achieved? In the development of the conceptual schema, the relationship between an antecedent variable and a subsequent variable had to be present in the literary use of the term. Once the schema has been constructed, however, the establishment of a relationship in each case is not as time bound.

This point becomes clear when we consider Future Adult Roles Relevance. We assume that content, teaching method, or learning method will be related in some way to the fulfillment of the student's future roles.

Although most school experiences are future-oriented, learning activities must be justified in their own right. But justification is not always a simple matter.

The issue of time has sharpened along with the increased demands for relevance. Many students do not want to be told that learning is good because it will help them in the future. They have no use for delayed gratification. Skeptical of adult wisdom, today's youth are not always convinced that such justifications have merit.

The deficiency of the future-oriented time frame is apparent when teachers present lectures to students and require them to take scrupulous notes on minute details because, teachers say, it prepares them for college. Unproductive and unstimulating experiences are being justified on the basis that the learner will have to engage in unproductive and unstimulating experiences in the future. Yet how many teachers are captive to this absurd logic?

At the other extreme is the emphasis on enjoyment and spontaneity now, regardless of future considerations. The pleasure principle that emphasizes today and disregards tomorrow can hardly be justified either.

Regardless of where the emphasis is placed—now or later—the educator should be aware of the goals he holds for the learning experience. Some intentions may be realized long after the experience is over (students may become active in civic affairs, for example). Other intentions may be realized at the time of the experience itself (students engage in critical thinking). In all cases, the learner ought to be aware of the intentions and even help formulate them.

An exception to the position that goals should be known at the time of the learning experience is represented by the category Self-generative Indeterminate Relevance. This category asserts the legitimacy of the learning experience that may affect each learner in unpredictable ways. A concert or any artistic presentation would be a prime example of this type of experience. On a more practical level, one student in a class of thirty may be so excited by his experiences in one course that he chooses to pursue similar experiences in the future. Choosing to be a scholar of classical languages or ancient history might be an appropriate example here. However, what about the other twenty-nine students who were not excited by their study? For them, the relevance may never have developed, and it would be fair to say that the course was irrelevant to their future adult lives, or psychological affective dimensions.

It is up to the teacher and students in each case to ascertain what level of uncertainty they can tolerate. Some teachers are all too content to live with uncertainty most of the time, and relevance is left too often to chance. Without knowing it, these teachers define relevance as self-generative and indeterminate. While admitting the validity of such a category, the conscientious teacher must ask himself whether this is indeed his intended strategy, or whether it exists by default. For the professional educator, the latter possibility is hardly defensible.

Other than present clear categories to assist the curricular planner in conceiving and announcing his intentions, the relevance framework does not resolve the question of time. The merit of a learning experience can be inferred from the relevance categories, but the moment when it is to be realized cannot. However, it is highly unlikely that experiences designed to be meaningful only at a future time would be able consistently to capture student imagination. When this is the case, then secondary and extrinsic rewards and punishments generally have to be resorted to.

It may be that unless the learner's senses are involved in a voluntary but committed manner (Psychological Affective Relevance), no other kinds of relevance have much chance of being achieved. As a noted leader in the field of humanistic education, Arthur Coombs, has noted:

> What affects human behavior . . . is not so much the forces exerted on people from without as the meanings existing for the individual within. It is feelings, beliefs, convictions, attitudes and understandings of the person who is behaving that constitutes the direction forces of behavior.[2]

In addition to this important insight, Coombs offers another approach to resolving the issue of time. Here it is important to draw a distinction between goals and objectives. Whereas goals resembling the relevance categories may be realized long after the learning experience itself, objectives for the learning experiences should be concerned with present accomplishments or performances. The educator's task, therefore, is to specify immediate objectives for the classroom that, when accomplished, offer the best evidence that progress toward the larger goals is being made. In terms of the relevance framework, the social studies educator needs to reduce each kind of relevance into a series of daily learning experiences that permit an observer to say "Yes, these activities relate to the learner's cognitive growth" (or basic human concerns, or public issues). In this way, the present activity is tied to immediate objectives that, in turn, form a path toward more distant goals.

Selection of Content

Turning again to the case of George Washington, we can reduce the issue to the question: How effective is the subject of George Washington for achieving particular kinds of relevance? It is in this area of content selection that the relevance schema can be most directly applied.

We found in Chapter 1 that practical outcomes often follow the use of educational slogans, however vague. One practical outcome, stemming from a desire to make social studies education more relevant, has been a strong emphasis on current events, often accompanied by the assertion that history is not relevant.

One problem here is the assumption that there is only one kind of social studies relevance—Society-oriented Public Issues Relevance—and that a focus on current events is the only way to achieve it. It fails to consider the many other kinds of relevance, and the many other avenues for achieving any one kind. For instance, Society-oriented Universal Human Experience Relevance or Society-oriented Cultural Values Relevance might be pursued through a study of historical civilizations or other cultures. Society-oriented Public Issues Relevance might be approached through the writings of Thomas Jefferson or Plato, and these may in fact contribute more to an understanding of current American society than analyses of current issues in the media.

As another example, consider the social studies department chairman who takes note of student apathy and recommends that teachers make their courses "more relevant." He then proposes that each course emphasize biographical studies because "kids really find a study of people relevant."

It may be that some students do find biographical studies particularly meaningful. However, if the department chairman was interested primarily in changing student attitudes (Psychological Affective Relevance), then varied strategies for reaching each and every student should be considered. On the other hand, if he believed that students would find a study of basic human concerns most meaningful (Universal Human Experience Relevance), then biographical studies might conceivably be one effective approach to that goal.

Let's look at the subject of history. In attempting to evaluate its potential for achieving kinds of relevance, two distinct approaches can be pursued. The first is to begin with history as the subject to be taught, and then determine: (1) What kinds of relevance can be emphasized effectively through a study of history? (2) What is it about the study of history that advances these kinds of relevance? For example, one history teacher might emphasize Society-oriented Cultural Values Relevance because he stresses the teaching of American values and institutions. Another teacher might see his objectives in terms of Society-oriented Public Issues Relevance and Learner-centered Psychological Cognitive Relevance because he focuses on the historical roots of current issues, and on the students' critical evaluation of the contending viewpoints. Yet another teacher may see no relationship between his course emphasis on comprehensive coverage of events and the kinds of relevance. In each of these cases, history is accepted as the beginning point and relevance is sought as an appropriate outcome.

A second approach to evaluating the value of history is to begin with the kinds of relevance, and then determine which social studies content areas and methodologies offer the most potential for achieving particular kinds of relevance. Then a study of history would have to be justified on the grounds that it was the most appropriate vehicle for reaching specific objectives.

For instance, suppose the members of a social studies department agreed that all of the kinds of relevance ought to be emphasized at one point or another in the curricular offerings. Their task would then be to plot out a set of content areas, each one holding the most promise for achieving a particular kind of relevance. In each case the question would be: What is the best way to achieve Cultural Values Relevance? Institutional Maintenance Relevance? and so forth. The criterion for teaching any subject area now becomes its estimated potential *vis a vis* specific objectives. Given this approach to planning, the value of a history course would have to be evaluated against that of anthropology, sociology, or psychology for every kind of relevance. Where history courses appeared most appropriate, they would justifiably be part of the curriculum.

As another example of the potential usefulness of the schema for curricular decisions, consider the following:

> The school administrators and teachers (of this district) have proposed the social studies curriculum be revamped to place less emphasis on traditional study of history and American "heroes." The new curriculum would incorporate more techniques of sociology and emphasize minority accomplishments. It would be more relevant to today's youth, its authors claim.[3]

If one placed the specific references about relevance into the diagrammatic framework used to develop the conceptual schema the result would be: techniques of sociology-minority accomplishments/relevant/today's youth. Placing this use within the schema could lead only to the vague designation Learner-centered Relevance. But the relevance schema can also be used as a heuristic tool for asking questions and for probing the broad context* for its particulars. For instance, we can ask why and how "techniques of sociology" and the emphasis on "minority accomplishments" are more relevant to today's youth. Also, to what in today's youth are these emphases supposed to be relevant?

To illustrate further applications of the relevance schema, let's examine a criticism of the same curriculum revision proposal.

> "The underlying philosophy of this report (proposal) might best be described as one of watered-down behaviorism, an unfortunate blend of

---

*Here the idea of *broad context* refers to the full situation within which the use of relevance occurred, rather than just to the sentences immediately surrounding the term.

disparate assumptions that take no account of the part played by human ideals, by passions and even by the fortuitous element in history . . .

"The impersonality of the approach is all the more to be regretted as school children can identify themselves much more easily with men than with movements, with personalities rather than with impersonal causes (on the exact nature of which experts moreover usually disagree)."[4]

Nowhere in this statement is the word *relevant* used, but the author presents some justification of why a study of the role of the personality in history is relevant to the learner (because "school children can identify themselves much more easily with men than with movements . . ."). In this case, the author emphasizes the precise relationship that he believes is important, rather than the relevance of the new curriculum.

As this example suggests, the relevance schema can be used to sift through claims of relevance for their particulars and to assess educational positions. By providing conceptual evidence that a claim of relevance might encompass several possibilities, the schema requires the educator to specify why one relationship is the most desirable.

If relationships important to social studies are being claimed but are not reflected in the schema, then the schema can be adjusted accordingly. The schema is always considered to be open and tentative; as new focuses for social studies instruction are emphasized, new kinds of relevance may emerge.

In this section, various examples were presented to show how the relevance schema can be used in decisions on content alternatives. However, it is one thing to identify a content area in terms of its relation to a kind of relevance, and quite another to determine how to put that relationship into practice. The relevance schema itself offers few obvious guidelines on methodological approaches. But certain applications might be identified that contribute to this important task.

Method of Instruction

The question of *how* to achieve kinds of relevance, as distinct from *what* kinds of relevance to emphasize, involves much more complex considerations. Let's suppose a teacher decides that Public Issues Relevance is the most appropriate objective for his course and students. The teacher could proceed to spend each class period lecturing to the students about current affairs, and requiring them to parrot back information. Any perceptive observer will see that this is little different from a focus upon any content area, at least in terms of teaching method and learning method.

It would appear that the matter of *how* as distinct from the *what* requires the instructional planner to blend together kinds of relevance. Why and how this occurs can be accounted for by the following reasoning.

Education is something that happens to a person. It does not consist of textbooks, bulletin boards, curriculum guides, or course outlines. Thus any intended outcomes must be realized through the individual experiences and growth of the learners.

Once this fact is accepted, then questions on how to achieve kinds of relevance can be approached more systematically. For instance, we have noted that regardless of what kind of society-oriented relevance is going to be emphasized, it must be pursued through an involvement of the learner. That is, Learner-centered Relevance is prerequisite to any other kind. Some of the more effective methods for achieving this goal involve:

1. blending the students' experiences outside of school with those in school (multi-media activities, attention to real problems and concerns, use of technology and community resources).
2. having the learner assume the role of active creator, as distinct from passive recipient, of materials (students can design media presentations, model representations, or set up learning areas).
3. using action-oriented learning experiences (simulations, role playing).
4. maintaining a classroom environment of truth and openness.
5. holding regular small group discussions.
6. giving students a voice in the decision-making processes.

The cognitive experience of each learner must also be plotted out in every instructional plan, regardless of the content focus. If a teacher consistently emphasizes only one or two mental operations, such as recall and comprehension, then the achievement of kinds of relevance, including Psychological Cognitive Relevance, is limited. Learner growth in varied and higher level intellectual operations must be encouraged in any instructional plan committed to educational relevance. (The teacher is advised to consult Bloom's *Taxonomy of Educational Objectives,* and design appropriate learning objectives and activities for each of the cognitive levels.)

As we consider the broad implications of the various relevance categories, it should become clear that the achievement of any one must be accompanied by a well-defined process dimension. Preparation for adult roles is more a matter of increasing one's thinking capabilities than of acquiring information and knowledge of procedures. Democracy is a process requiring decision-making skills rather than a set of facts. It is important for the student to study public issues in order to learn how to confront issues on his own—today and later as an adult. The study of human experiences is vital because it gives the learner a deeper understanding of his own humanity.

The two other learner-centered categories (Contiguous Environmental Relevance and Future Adult Roles Relevance) might be viewed as further avenues for changing a learner's behavior. That is, one strategy for influencing a learner's attitude and provoking thought is to relate the instruction to his immediate sphere of activity. Another is to relate it to his future needs. In both cases, the meaningfulness of the instruction is clear, and the learner's senses readily captured.

The methodological dimension of an instructional plan, therefore, is contained in the learner-centeredness of that plan. Relevance can be achieved to the extent that the learner grows.

Evaluating for Relevance

When a social studies teacher or curricular planner decides on the kinds of relevance to emphasize, he is committing the program to definite objectives. The degree of attainment of these objectives constitutes one evaluative task.

Once the objectives are specified, the next task is to identify alternative strategies for achieving the objectives. (Various examples of instructional strategies were presented in the examples discussed in this chapter.) In pursuing any particular strategy, the evaluator should be concerned with the question: How well is the program moving toward the objectives? This question contains a commitment to an ongoing evaluation effort. This is different from an evaluation based on the question: How well did I do?

When an evaluation is concerned primarily with gathering data in order to improve a program, it is called *formative evaluation.*[5] When evaluation is concerned with securing data for a terminal judgment on the worth of a program, it is called *summative evaluation.* Both types are important in trying to determine whether relevance is being achieved.

Evaluation concerned with program improvement must have a strong monitoring dimension so that particular decisions and activities can be assessed for their effectiveness in accomplishing specific objectives. When a discrepancy can be detected between what is planned and what is actually occurring, then the program should be modified accordingly.

Another evaluation model[6] is based on the view that the purpose of education is to judge decision alternatives. To evaluate, therefore, it is necessary to know the alternatives to be judged and the criteria for judging them. Using the relevance schema, the social studies instructor has clear conceptual guidelines for alternative courses. He can decide what direction(s) to pursue, and what criteria he will accept as evidence that he is making progress. Each kind of relevance thus represents a possible decision, and each requires its own evaluative design.

One other consideration needs to be brought out, and it relates to the time element. How does one evaluate a program when its goals are future-oriented? Here the important understanding is that, although goals may not be realized for years, program objectives need to be defined in such a way as to be realizable in the present. Thus the criteria on whether a kind of relevance is being achieved must define performance levels or conditions that can be attained in the current program.

Although considerations for evaluation conclude this analysis of relevance in social studies education, evaluation is not necessarily the final task. The position we have adopted throughout this book has consistently stressed the openness of both conceptual and learning models, and the necessity for continuous feedback and modification. But the issues raised by demands for relevance require a wide range of educational skills—from clarifying the implications of educational concepts to determining whether program implementation is consistent with decisions. To seek educational relevance is to seek educational excellence in all of its manifestations.

Notes

1. Stone, *op. cit.,* pp. 528–532.
2. Arthur Coombs, from *Seeing is Behaving* as quoted in "Conversation: Two Humanists," *Media & Methods,* December 1971, p. 24.
3. As quoted in *Palo Alto Times,* 4 August 1970.
4. *Ibid.*
5. Michael Scriven, "The Methodology of Evaluation," in *Perspectives in Curriculum Evaluation,* ed. B. O. Smith (Chicago: Rand McNally, 1967), pp. 39–83.
6. D. L. Stufflebeam and E. G. Guba, eds., *Educational Evaluation and Decision Making.* Report by the Phi Delta Kappa National Study Commission on Evaluation, (1971).

POSTSCRIPT

Now that we have identified the kinds of relevance for social studies, described their selection, and discussed their application, we can step back to examine some of the underlying questions from a broader perspective.

Question: Why can't uses of relevance in social studies or any other context simply be divided into two categories—the slogan use and the dictionary use?

The justification for particular kinds of relevance resides in the specification of a context. The references themselves are the critical factor. Thus, the conceptual schema on kinds of relevance for social studies demands relationships between specific social studies variables. To accept any focuses for the antecedent variables apart from those comprising the established social studies categories would be inappropriate in light of the objective regarding the specific implications of relevance for social studies.

Question: Recognizing that the schema's development depends on the identification and categorization of the references about relevance, isn't the schema more properly a conceptualization of social studies variables than of "kinds of relevance" for social studies? That is, why aren't the conclusions stated in terms of conceptualizing focuses for relevance rather than kinds of relevance?

These two outcomes are not separate considerations, but are in fact the same. Although the exact references were the most important criteria in constructing the conceptual schema, the word *relevant* itself depends on its references to communicate specific meaning. But by clarifying the

67

references about uses of relevance within the context of social studies education, the focuses for the antecedent instructional variables are also clarified. Thus, the process of conceptualizing uses of relevance in social studies has resulted in the conceptualization of focuses or objectives for social studies education.

Question: **Recognizing that a conceptualization of kinds of relevance for social studies has also led to a conceptualization of social studies objectives, what can we say about the status of** relevance **as an educational concept? Has** relevance **been elevated to the position of a concept where it communicates educational meaning by itself, as in** a relevant curriculum?

The primary conclusion that can be drawn from the conceptual schema is that relevance entails multiple implications for social studies education. This argues against a use of relevance as though it alone communicated specific meaning. However, we can give general interpretations to relevance drawing upon the results presented here. One interpretation says that the term relevance can be used in an educational context to convey a demand for specific intentions, goals, or consequences. Irrelevant education is aimless; relevant education has some clear purposes. A relevant curriculum is one with definite intentions or objectives.

A second general meaning can be inferred from the phrase "capturing the learner's senses." There is little doubt that *educational relevance* implies a particular effect upon a learner by some instructional elements. The learner is involved, aroused, and committed. The nature of this commitment is not at all obvious, but it must be demonstrated before relevance can be claimed.

Assigning various interpretations to relevance imparts some legitimacy to the term as an educational concept. However, to say that relevance is just one more general expression (synonymous with goals or objectives or learner motivation) is to say that it communicates little, if any, substantive educational meaning.

The conclusion that relevance *per se* has little importance as an educational concept does not speak to the conceptual schema on kinds of relevance. We can conclude that relevance, conceptualized into its multiple possibilities, does have the potential to effect action in the social studies.

APPENDIX

In order to clarify further the practical applications of the conceptual schema of kinds of relevance for social studies, examples of instructional objectives and learning activities are presented in this section. Hopefully the classroom teacher will see how specific instructional approaches can be derived from the conceptual schema, and conclude his investigation into relevance and the social studies with some practical suggestions in hand.

The objectives and activities presented here are representative of selected kinds of relevance for social studies. Although the list is not exhaustive, the examples are sufficiently representative of the schema's possibilities that further combinations would be redundant.

Learner-controlled Relevance

Objective: Each student will identify one question within the context of the subject under study that he wishes to pursue in depth.

Student Activities:

- List as many questions as you can think of within the context of the course. Identify the three that you are most interested in. From the final list, select one that you wish to pursue as a personal assignment.
- Skim the main sections of a textbook or a chapter—section headings, picture captions, and summaries—and list questions that can be raised from the material.

Learner–controlled and Non-learner–controlled Relevance

(*Note:* Because these two categories are often combined in actual practice, they are also combined here.)

Objective: Through decision-making experiences within limits established by the teacher, the student will grow in the skills and attitudes of self-determination.

Student Activities:

- Help to identify course objectives by discussing your expectations for the course, and the areas in which you would like to study and grow personally.
- From a list of research topics, choose the topics you wish to investigate and report on.

Psychological Cognitive Relevance

Objective: Students will grow in their abilities to analyze and evaluate social studies concepts.

Student Activities:

- Given one interpretation of an issue central to the course (*Example:* an editorial on a current issue, an historian's interpretation explaining events of the past, or a sociologist's explanation of current social phenomena), identify the author's main idea or thesis and list its strengths and weaknesses. Present your own summary evaluation of the material.
- Given a series of key decisions in an historical era or in a current

controversy, complete the following statement for each decision: I think that (decision in question) was a good/bad decision because_____

_____ .

Objective: Students will practice divergent thinking.

Student Activities:

- Given an open-ended problem, identify as many solutions or possible outcomes as you can. Then develop a total group set of solutions or possible outcomes. (At first, this activity could also be conducted through small group problem-solving or brain-storming rather than by individual efforts.)
- Given a collection of related data, or a description of some experience, work in a small group to develop an interpretation for the data or experience. Now compare your group's product with those of the other groups. Through discussion, attempt to account for the differences.

Psychological Affective Relevance

Objective: Students will develop a commitment to learning that is based on intrinsic rather than extrinsic rewards.

Student Activities:

- Identify your primary interests and talents within the context of the course, although those falling outside of the immediate course context should be considered as well. Then, in conjunction with the teacher, develop activities and assignments which allow you to pursue your own interests and talents. (*Example:* A student with a talent for sketching can draw some cartoons or caricatures on course subjects, or students with an interest in theatre can write and present dramatic episodes to the class.)
- Discuss with the teacher your progress toward course objectives, and your growth in personal skills and attitudes. Discuss with the class ways that the course can be improved in terms of learning opportunities and development.

Objective: Students will clarify their own values regarding social, economic, and personal issues.

Student Activities:

- Given a series of case studies that involve controversies, decide how you think each case should be resolved, then analyze the other students' positions, clarifying the values dominant in each case.

- Given a list of areas where the federal government could invest more or less of its funds, identify the decisions you would make with regard to the allocation of the funds. Next, analyze your decisions for their value implications.
- Describe a Utopian society, showing how it would differ from the present U.S. society. Analyze your description for value implications.
- First, identify your most important personal values. Then explain how you spend your weeks, describing the activities that take up your time. Compare the two lists to determine whether your activities are consistent with your stated values. Discuss whether values reside more in statements or in actions.

Contiguous Environmental Relevance

Objective: Students will be able to draw upon and relate their own personal experiences in studying course content.

Student Activities:

- Identify issues or topics that are important in your community, neighborhood, family, or personal life. With the teacher, build units of study based on these areas of concern.
- Hold class discussions, preferably in small groups of ten to fifteen students, to consider topics of personal concern to you and other students. Express your personal feelings and ideas.

Objective: Students will be able to relate the concepts and experiences of the course to their own personal lives.

Student Activities:

- For each important concept stressed in the course, discuss personal experiences in which the concept is involved.
- Write a brief explanation of what a concept or class experience means to you personally.

Objective: Students will be able to better utilize the resources of the community in course activities and assignments.

Student Activities:

- Undertake a class, group, or individual project that leads to some service being performed for the community or persons within the community. (*Example:* Students might present a petition to the city government showing citizen support for the addition of some new safety feature in a neighborhood, volunteer their time to tutor mentally retarded children, or work with mentally ill patients.)

- Have students gather data from their own neighborhood or community and have them use the data as the basis for a research report. (*Example:* Investigate pricing differences in local stores, or attitudes regarding community or school issues.)

Future Adult Roles Relevance

Objective: Course experiences will prepare students for the responsibilities and roles they will assume in the future.

Student Activities:

- Simulate selected adult roles regarding issues of current or future importance (*Example:* construction of a dam that will create a large lake and obliterate a canyon of natural splendor).
- Study various representations of future possibilities. Then consider the question, what should the future be like? Identify decisions or courses of action that needed to be pursued now in order to make the future take shape as you want it to.
- Choose to investigate and report on one of the following topics: (a) the purchase of a car on credit, (b) the purchase of a home, (c) the investment of a sum of money in stocks, (d) the start of a new business, or (e) the allocation of a family budget.

Public Issues Relevance

Objective: Students will develop their abilities of reflective thinking on issues of current significance, and formulate conclusions of their own on the issues in question.

Student Activities:

- Identify five major issues that are of national significance. By yourself or with a group select one issue and identify, through research, the spectrum of contending viewpoints on the issue. With the others, discuss the various positions. Then develop your own position on the issue, emphasizing the strength of your justification of this position.
- Listen as two teachers present two contending points of view on an issue. The teachers should debate their viewpoints and respond to student questions.

- Practice role playing, by taking the positions of leading spokesmen on an issue of current import.

Universal Human Experience Relevance

Objective: Students will comprehend the universality of human traits, attitudes, feelings, and states of being.

Student Activities:

- Find good portrayals in historical literature of the following human traits: courage, fear, hate, prejudice, compassion, sorrow, bravery, love, trust, suspicion, and unselfishness.
- Study at least three other civilizations, cultures, or sub-cultures, and identify the major similarities and differences in the way people live (*Example:* Asian countries, African civilizations, island cultures, Mexican-American culture, or American Indian tribes.)
- Discuss the following questions: (a) Is war an inevitable condition of man? (b) How does increasing technological development affect all peoples? (c) What do all people share in common?

Cultural Values Relevance

Objective: Students will understand the concept of cultural values, and how one culture is apt to have values that are different from those of another.

Student Activities:

- List the beliefs, ideas, and practices that most Americans hold most important or follow consistently in their lives. Discuss these in relation to the concept of value.
- Analyze, through class discussion, the values that schools are transmitting.
- Discuss how the values of your generation differ from those of your parents' generation.
- Study other cultures throughout the world, especially those that are primitive by technological standards. Compare the values of these cultures with those of the dominant white middle-class American culture.

Institutional Maintenance Relevance

Objective: Students will develop skills and attitudes necessary for the continuance of American institutions.

Student Activities:

- Identify the main requirements on the part of people for (a) a democratic government, (b) a multi-cultural society, (c) a free enterprise economic system. Then identify the skills and attitudes necessary for the successful functioning of these institutions and characteristics of our society. Discuss whether courses in school are equipping you with those skills and attitudes.
- Discuss ways that major changes can be produced in this nation. Consider the role of dissent in a democracy, or how violence (*Example:* political assassinations) thwarts democratic processes.
- Hold mock elections, Congressional hearings, Supreme Court deliberations, or United Nations sessions.

STAFFORD LIBRARY
COLUMBIA COLLEGE
COLUMBIA, MO 65216

Columbia College
Columbia, Missouri